Amazon ISBN: 9781695278400

This e-book has been written to provide information about making it safely and successful in the Music Business. Every effort has been made to make this e-book as complete and accurate as possible. While all attempts have been made to verify information provided in this publication, the author and publisher assumes no responsibility for errors, omissions, or contrary interpretation of the subject matter herein. The purpose of this e-book is to educate. This eBook is thus for informational purposes only and is not intended for use as a source of legal, business, financial or professional advice. All readers are advised to seek services of competent professionals in legal, business, finance, and relevant fields. Therefore, this eBook should be used as a guide - not as the ultimate source.

Artist Development & Management Course

Contents

Section 1:

The Artist Looks for A Manager

(<u>Note:</u> "You" equals "Artist" - this section)

1. What Does a Professional Manager Do?

A. A Manager is a person or company, who guides, counsels, advises and helps to provide employment.

B. He/she/they are a protector, and "doer".

C. They take all steps necessary to help you become a success.

D. They make money when you make money; the more you make, the more they make. Their success comes through helping you to achieve your success.

E. They can be an objective person who can look at all aspects of your situation, analyze them, and make a rational plan. They have to be able to look at you and your work differently than you do. Why?

   1. Your work is intensely personal, and you're probably too emotionally tied to it.

   2. Everyone needs a professional outside opinion, not friends or relatives. It's hard for them to give an honest, sound opinion.

      a. They're too close to be honest and objective.

      b. If they're not professionals, they're not qualified to give an opinion.

c. If you listen only to friends and those close to you, you'll run around in circles, being pleased with yourself without making any progress. Or worse, they don't like your stuff, or they're jealous - and you and your Music really have "hit music" potential!

Do not mix up the terms "Manager" and "Agent" - many people do! They are two different animals. Agents are "middle-men/women" who get "gigs" etc., for people. Managers, as you will see in the contract in "Section Two", may hire Agents for you when needed.

Agents often need an "Employment Agency License" to legally do their work. Managers cannot legally "book" Artists, although some will book their Artists here and there, in the beginning.

2. When You May Need a Manager

A. When you've reached a certain, good level on your own, and can't seem to progress any higher, no matter what you do.

The top Managers won't touch you until you reach a pretty good level on your own. You need to look like, and actually be a business up-and-running!

B. When you may have no idea what you should do, or do next.

C. You may be disorganized, lost, or simply not have the right contacts to get ahead any further. You realize you're spinning your wheels and going nowhere.

3. When You Don't Need A Manager

A. If you're solely a Songwriter and not an Artist.

B. You're happy being a local Band, or Group. Look into getting an "Agent", instead, if you wish, to help you.

C. When you're just starting out.

4. Why May You Need A Manager?

A. "I don't need a Manager; I can do it all myself." That's not a good way of thinking, though you may be able to do it for a while, until you feel you're ready to really move ahead. Your major time should be focused on your Music and your Fans!

B. Strong musical, writing or singing talent does not necessarily mean you have good managerial ability.

C. Your time is better spent creatively, constantly improving what you do.

D. Do you really know what the best move is that you can make?

E. Do you actually have an honest evaluation of your own work? Can you be objective about it?

5. Attributes Of A Top, Professional Manager

A. Has contacts in the music industry.

Remember: It's not just whom they know, but more importantly - who knows them!

B. Knows what's happening in the industry – at the present time.

C. Knows what Booking Agents, Publishers, Record Companies and any other would-be interested people or companies would be looking for.

D. Probably has (should have) experience managing others.

E. Knows the advantages and pitfalls in almost every situation that's likely to arise.

F. Is "streetwise" in dealing in the industry.

G. Can avoid blind alleys in negotiations, make fewer mistakes, and save you time and money.

H. "Takes the heat off you" from your attorney, Band Members or Group, Club Owners and Managers, Booking Agents, Record Company exec.'s, etc. That is, they play "the bad guy" for you.

Many artists have killed either their recording or performing careers by fighting over assorted issues, either musically or business oriented. Your Manager, not you, is the one to fight with the company or person! They can be the super tough "bad guy", or turn around and play "good guy" for you.

I. Is totally up-to-date and knows and understands the "Digital Revolution" including the formats and their uses.

J. Knows a lot about branding, marketing and promotion, including the Web and keeps up with the latest technologies and techniques to stay a step ahead....

They can do so many things for you, if they're great. If they aren't, you'll curse the day you met them. But also keep in mind, no one has every quality you and others might think necessary, but they should be able to make up for any important weaknesses by associating with others who can fill in the missing pieces.

6. How do you find a great Manager?

The same rules apply as for the other important people involved in your career. But you must be even more careful in this case, however, because of the would-be Managers who'll do you more harm than good, if you fall for the "spiel" about how great you are, and/or what they can accomplish for you.

A. Personal Managers may be "staff people" - that is, part of a larger Management Company.

1. One person may be the designated "Manager", but may be backed up by a large, professional organization that can literally do anything to promote the Artist's career.

2. They generally control every aspect of the Artist's career.

3. The Management Company can provide certain advantages an independent Manager might not be able to handle. For instance,

a. They might be able to advance some money to help you build your career and increase your income.

You should realize that any money they advance towards your career has to come back to them, plus a profit, or they're not going to do it. You could conceivably be a "rising star" for some time before you're getting all the money you should because they are paying themselves back.

b. They most probably have movie and TV "friends", and may even be able to help produce a network TV show for you, etc.

Due to their interest in "slimming down" their staff, many Record Companies have been scaling back on their staff and are expecting more out of Managers, including many services that used to be covered by the Labels, plus dealing with all the new kinds of opportunities presenting themselves quite often with new technologies.

4. One problem some artists have with this arrangement is the organization itself seems impersonal. This can be very irritating to some Artists due to the fact that they are often sensitive people by nature.

5. If you can't sustain the success, you may not be worth the effort to them, and they may not put a lot of effort out for you - even though you're still under contract.

B. Personal Managers may be Independent Proprietors.

1. You may feel more comfortable having a really "personal" Personal Manager, so that your discussions go no further, and are not subjected to "executive review" as they often are in a management company. The Personal Manager, unlike the big companies, does not tend to operate by "formula", and may be more attentive to you.

2. You want the "team feeling", and have the need to feel more secure.

C. There are three managerial styles of Personal Managers:

1. The "Boss" type, where they tell you what to do, and expect you to do it.

2. The "Team" type, where you discuss everything together and come to a decision.

3. You are the Boss, and they do what you want them to do.

There may be a problem with the Team type, when there is a "tie vote". Somebody has to have the final decision - and in my opinion, in most cases, it should be the Manager - that's why you hired them. Or, you can have a mutually agreed upon 3rd party help mediate any sticky situations.

Unless you know the Biz inside and out, I do not recommend the Artist is the Boss.

Which of the three are more worth it? Only you know the answer. My opinion? Take videos & recordings to all types of Managers, and see what their response is, and then decide.

7. Choosing your Manager

Important Note: As much care should be taken in finding a Manager, as in finding a partner for marriage. You will in effect be "married" to this person for some time, usually at least several years, and the "divorce" might even be more difficult to achieve and settle than one from a regular marriage. If it works, finding a Manager could possibly be the single most positive important career decision you make.

A. It's important to remember, you must choose the correct **Person** or **Company** to manage your career.

This is probably the most important decision in your professional life. You may be giving away control over your career, and essentially your life, for an extended period of time.

B. There are two key considerations that will <u>not</u> appear in any contract:

1. "Can you trust this Person?" - You must have complete trust in them because:

a. A "Power of Attorney" contract clause is involved. This means they can sign your name to many, if not all legal agreements, and you will be bound by them.

Always have this adjusted if it gives them complete power - more on this later.

b. They will, initially, most probably, be handling all of your money.

2. *"Can* this Person advance my career?"

"Great intentions" do not make a great Manager. He/she may have the best, most sincere intent in the world, and really want to help make you an outstanding success. But, to do this they:

a. Must have knowledge of the industry,

b. Contacts within it,

c. Prestige, and

d. Power & influence.

C. What should you do to make sure they are right for you?

1. Check them out within the industry.

2. Have them give references and check them.

3. Ask others they manage.

4. Ask Artists they once managed and find out why they aren't still together. (Evaluate these reasons. The Manager may not have been at fault!)

5. Have someone who really knows the Industry, such as an Entertainment Attorney, "grill them" for you.

D. You may find you like this person, and believe in them and their abilities, although you may feel they have some shortcomings. Weigh these things out and make a decision. Remember that you may be "together" for a long time!

E. You should feel that your potential Manager has the desire and is ready to move your career forward.

They should give you a general idea of what they will do, on some kind of schedule, and how long it will take to get started. Forget the ones that say, "Well, if I tell you, you won't need me!" or the like.

F. Don't confuse "style" with "ability". They may seem too "laid back" and easy-going for you. Or they may appear to be too "manic". As long as they have the abilities brought up in this lesson it doesn't matter how they do something - only whether it gets done, and done well!

G. Remember that <u>a contract is only as good as the people who sign it</u>. Many persuasive people "talk" a good job, but when they have to, can't. Be sure this applies neither to your Personal Manager nor yourself, because it takes both to make it work.

At this point in time, I will touch on two other types of Managers involved in an Artist's career

---

8. The Road Manager

A. When you're playing away from home, you might require the services of a "Road Manager" (often called a "Tour Manager"). Simply put, a Road Manager is the Manager on the road...

I'm discussing the role of the Road Manager with the understanding that, maybe at first, you may just have to use some friends to help out, and it'll probably work out ok, especially for local and regional performances, etc. And yes, the Band members may have to help, also.

But there will come a time when you need a real professional with all the experience and knowledge necessary to handle completely complex situations...

1. Not everyone has what it takes to be a great Road Manager.

    a. It's loaded with all kinds of responsibility.

    b. It's demanding of time and energy.

B. Since it is such an all-around job that varies from Performer to Performer, Group to Group, Tour to Tour, I will have to generalize in describing it. So, in general, this person must be responsible for:

1. Organizing your travel from beginning to end.

2. Making sure you get where you have to be, on time, and without any avoidable snags or hang-ups.

3. Taking charge of lodging.

4. Stage setup.

5. Moving and setting up equipment, both sound and lighting.

6. Making sure there's proper security for equipment and security personnel as needed.

7. Being in charge of the Roadies, and Merchandise People, including hiring them if necessary, choosing those that will be able to do their job, and do it well.

8. Dealing with financial issues and collecting the money.

9. Keeping in contact with your Personal Manager, who probably will be taking care of other important things from home base.

Some Personal Managers also travel with Artists or Groups/Bands as Road Manager, at least in the beginning.

The Artist should not have to do or worry about anything other than performing, treating their fans well, doing interviews and other related promo things. Traveling is wearing enough without having to worry about details concerning it.

C. Professional Road Managers are prepared for any situation, from securing drum repairs in Cleveland, to finding a pair of the right sized colored or patterned stockings in Philadelphia at 10PM, for example.

1. They love challenges! The joy of their life is making everything run smoothly despite any problems that may arise.

2. Great Road Managers are in the running for the "Master Go-fer" title.

Your smooth, successful touring is largely their doing. They should be properly appreciated because their part in making the Performer(s) successful may be unseen, but is tremendously important. If you find a great one, take care of them for taking care of you!

D. They usually are paid a weekly salary.

9. The Business Manager

Performers are generally Performers, rather than experts in the field of finance, and some have met with disastrous results trying to handle their own money. It depends, of course, on the individual, and what he/she feels is best.

A. Simply put, the Business Manager looks after the Artist's money.

1. A Business Manager takes over the part of your Personal Manager's job that is involved in collecting and taking care of your money for you. In part, this person will often:

a. Invest your money

b. Pay your bills

c. Work out your "pocket money"

d. Advise and work with you on your tax situation.

2. He/she can be:

a. An accountant

b. An investment counselor

c. An attorney (usually a tax specialist)

d. Someone you know is really good at business, and you feel you can trust with your money.

B. If he/she/they have been recommended to you, or have come to your attention, check them out very, very carefully before proceeding into a contractual arrangement. You will be entrusting this person with your hard-earned money!

C. Draw up a contract that specifies:

1. What points are to be covered.

2. The extent of authority they have.

3. An inspection of the account books - to be maintained in your best interest, at least every six months.

4. That you are to be filled in on every deal, every investment, before anything is done - and they only have the power to act in these situations, with your prior written approval.

Remember: You have hired a Business Manager to manage your business, not to exclude you from it!

Section 2:

Artist Management Negotiations
("you" = "Artist", again, this section)

Important Note: *Before you even entertain the thought of hiring a Manager, please check out "**Addendum #1**" at the end of this course. Then, once you're sure you've taken care of everything in that Addendum which you possibly can, and you believe you've found the <u>right</u> person or Company, the time has come...*

1. Meeting with Your Manager

You've made your decision - you've picked a Manager. Now, sit down and discuss with the Manager your career goals, strengths and weaknesses.

1. Don't "gloss over" your shortcomings

2. Don't overplay your strengths.

3. Do be factual and honest. Managers have to know the Artist at least as well as the Artist knows him-, her- or themselves.

2. The Artist/Management Contractual Agreement

Important Notes:

A. Do not give or sell this contract or any of its contents to anyone - it is for educational use only. A contract in the wrong hands can be very dangerous to someone's career!

B. Please note: This is a "basic contract" that can be "worked from", like a "template." It is not a complete agreement because it has not been personalized for a particular person, group or situation, and there are important points left out of it that would make it legal and fair, plus it's "dated". I would NEVER use this contract as is - whether I was representing the Artist *or* the Manager!

C. You should always go to a Music Business Contract Specialist, like I am, a Music Business Consultant with 35 years' experience writing and negotiating contracts, or to an Entertainment Attorney well versed and up to date in the Music Biz regarding any Music Business Contracts, to ensure you are being properly protected!

D. As you probably have seen, the business has been changing extremely rapidly and radically in the last few years, both in the way everything is handled, let alone the new technologies and formats appearing, and what that can mean regarding your career.

In the following Contract the...

→ Bold print = my thoughts, opinions, explanations following the phrase or sentence(s) or "(fill-ins)". They will be in brackets: ( )'s:

→ Plain print = actual original contract words

STANDARD MANAGEMENT AGREEMENT

(There Is No Such Thing As A "Standard Management", Or Any Other Type Agreement! Always ignore the word "Standard" and act like it wasn't there!)

AGREEMENT made and entered into in the **(City or Town)** of **(Name of City or Town)**, **(Commonwealth or State)** of

(Name of Commonwealth or State), this **(Day Number)** day of **(Month)**, **(Year)**, by and between **(Name of Manager or Management Company)** (hereinafter referred to as Manager) and **(Legal Name of Artist and any aliases)** (hereinafter referred to as Artist).

(Note: If there are 2 people in a group, both people are listed individually, and it will state as follows: __Name__ and __Name__ (individually and jointly hereinafter referred to as Artist);

If there are 3 people in group, each person is listed individually and it will state as follows: __Name__, and __Name_, and Name_ (individually, jointly and collectively hereinafter referred to as Artist)

If there are 4 or more people in group, each person is listed individually and it will state as follows: __Name__, and __Name_, and Name_, and Name (individually, jointly, severally and collectively hereinafter referred to as Artist))

Whereas, Artist desires to obtain counsel, advice, guidance and employment in the entertainment industry; and

Whereas, Manager desires to furnish said counsel, advice, guidance and employment on behalf of artist.

(Did you notice there's "desire" not "promises". Actually nobody can promise an Artist "stardom", but there should be a "strong desire" evident"!)

Now therefore, the parties hereto, intending to be legally bound mutually agree as follows:

1. Artist hereby employs Manager's services as Artist's exclusive personal manager...

(you'll notice the word "exclusive" - which means this Manager is the only person who can act in the capacity of Artist's Manager as described in this Agreement)

...with respect to all of Artist's activities in the entertainment industries including, but not limited to: nightclubs, theatrical engagements, fairs, road shows, tours, and all personal appearances; motion pictures,...

(Motion pictures? Yes, even if Artist has no inclination at present, you never know. . . Also, keep in mind, the Artist might never have received a film offer without Manager helping Artist "make it" in music, first!),

...television, radio and all other productions; phonograph records, prerecorded tapes and all other sound and audiovisual recordings; musical compositions, and all other writings; publishing; endorsements, commercial merchandising, tie-ins, and all other commercial use of Artist's name, likeness, and other aspects of Artist's personality.

(In plain, simple language, the Artist is tied to Manager, financially and otherwise, in _any_ and _everything_ regarding the entire _Entertainment_ Business)

2. It is understood and agreed that Artist is so employing Manager because of her desire to increase her earning capacity as an Artist which Manager represents he shall be able to do, because Manager shall expend money...

(when it says "expend money... as hereafter provided" - it means money only will be spent on Artist by Manager if, and how it's stated in contract! Many Artists look to Manager as somebody who will invest whatever money is necessary on them - but that is _not_ a listed part of Manager's "job", in most cases! Although some Managers spend a little to keep

things moving, most Managers spend close to nothing on Artists)

...and effort as hereafter provided...

(regarding "and effort as hereafter provided", keep in mind that in most cases, what the Manager is supposed to do is often neither listed nor clear.)

...on Artist's behalf in any and every way consistent with proper managerial employment.

3. Manager agrees that he will use all reasonable efforts...

("*reasonable* efforts"? - who decides what's "reasonable"? Most lawyers will automatically change "all reasonable efforts" to "his (or her) <u>best</u> efforts")

...to further promote, develop and advance Artist's professional career in her best interests, and to confer with, counsel and advise her in all matters and things related thereto. Manager further agrees that on Artist's behalf, Manager will negotiate, counsel and confer with booking agencies, employers and other users of entertainment, and that Manager will supervise and advise her concerning all professional material and billing. Manager agrees that he will counsel and advise Artist in all matters and things concerning her professional career for the purpose of exploiting and enhancing her commercial value.

4. Artist does not look to Manager to procure or provide engagements for her or to act as a booking agent in her behalf.

(Do not mix up the roles of "Manager" and "Agent". It's amazing how many acts look for a Manager to get gigs, when what they're really looking for is an Agent, who, by the way, in most states, must have an "Employment Agency license". Matter of fact, it's often illegal to do both, with the

exception that there's not usually any problem if kept on a limited, local scale when dealing with their own Artist(s), only.)

However, Artist understands that Manager shall employ a booking agent or booking agents in her behalf whose commissions shall be paid for by Artist.

5. Artist understands that Manager is or may be engaged in a similar capacity for other persons, businesses or corporations, and Artist agrees that Manager is not obligated to devote his time and attention exclusively to the Artist.

(As you can see, Manager is <u>not</u> signed exclusively to Artist!)

Artist acknowledges that Manager may have an ownership interest in a music publishing company and/or in a phonograph recording company, or that Manager may receive Producer's royalties from a recording company, with which Artist may enter into an exclusive contract, and acknowledges that same is not inconsistent with Manager's duties or right to compensation hereunder.

(It is becoming quite common for a Manager to wear many "hats" nowadays. For example, they may want to be Artist's Manager, Producer, Publisher - and even their Record Company! All at once!

Give this some serious thought! There are 3 serious things to think about:

1. How can the Artist trust their Manager, for example, to check out and motivate their Record Company, if their Manager <u>is</u> their Record Company! (Possible conflict of interest)

2. Will they have the time to do multiple jobs, let alone do them well! And,

3. Do they really have the expertise to do them all!!!)

Note: Artist should seriously think about owning their own Publishing & Record Companies, and merely having the Manager oversee them.

Manager shall inform Artist of the name of any said company and acknowledges that Artist has no obligation to enter into any agreement with any such company described above.

(This final sentence at least makes Manager make the Artist aware of their possible intentions - and gives the Artist a choice!)

6. Artist hereby represents and warrants that she has no outstanding agreement, nor has she made any other arrangements, oral or written, which shall in any manner interfere with or prevent her from carrying out the terms and conditions of this Agreement.

(As a Manager, the first thing I would ask an Artist if I'm interested in them in any way is: "Have you ever been signed to anyone before for <u>anything</u>?" Often a person thinks that another Agreement they signed doesn't affect them, but it actually may; or they believe they are out of a contract - when actually they are not!

I, as a Manager, would ask to see <u>any </u>contract they've <u>ever </u>signed. I've also run into several cases where the Artist thought time had expired, but in actuality, according to the contract, it hadn't even legally <u>started</u> yet!!!

Artists, if there is any question, get <u>a written and signed release</u> releasing you from any future obligations of any nature from that old person or company!!!)

She further agrees that she will not, during the term hereof, engage any other person, firm or corporation, to act in the capacity of personal manager, representative or advisor.

(This may get interesting, nowadays, when an Artist also signs a Production Company Agreement with someone else, where that Company also requests that <u>they</u> are the sole advisor and representative! If this is true, Manager and Production Company must come to some form of agreement. For example, Producer can make a deal with the Record Company, but Manager must okay the deal, looking out for his Artist's best interests.)

This Agreement shall supersede any former agreements that may exist between Manager and Artist.

(This means that, if Manager promised something would be in the contract, for example, and it isn't in the contract - it doesn't count. Or, if they've signed a previous Agreement together, this piece of paper is what counts. Therefore, make sure what Manager promises, and what is actually in the contract, are the same)

7. Artist agrees to refer to Manager all verbal or written leads, communications or requests for Artist's appearances and services,

(If I were the Artist, I would want it to say "Artist and Manager agree to refer *to each other*..." This section of the clause helps ensure that each party knows what's going on behind their back.

Any deals that involve Artist, in any way, directly or indirectly, are to be fully explained with prior approval given by the other party before any major deal is made. This helps negate the chance of "side deals" whereby only one side profits.

And let's face it – you're supposed to be a Team! You should each know what the other is doing!)

and Artist agrees that Manager may publicly represent himself as acting for Artist in the capacity herein set forth.

(This part of the clause is very important for the Manager or anyone representing the Artist. Nobody should act as an Artist's representative when looking for any kind of deal, without the written consent of the Artist! Wicked problems could occur!)

For this purpose, Manager shall have the right to use Artist's photograph and her name for advertising materials, and to authorize others to use Artist's name and photograph in such manner as Manager may deem advisable.

(Most Artists prefer to have the right to approve of any promotional or marketing material being used. This can affect an Artist's "Image" which is very important – all people promoting Artist should stay within the Image guidelines.)

8. Artist hereby appoints Manager, her true and lawful attorney during the term of this Agreement, to sign and make on Artist's behalf all agreements in connection with all engagements and arrangements contemplated herein whereby her name, likeness, services or talents are mentioned, referred to or utilized.

(Simply put, this is called a "Power-of-Attorney" clause, giving the Manager the right to sign the Artist's name to anything. And, as you will see in the next sentence in this clause, the Artist will have to follow through on what they signed up for.

Now referring back to #5, with a Power-of Attorney Clause, the Artist can sign them to them as their Manager, and <u>Manager can sign the Artist's name to their own Record or Publishing Companies</u>!!! The Artist must <u>always</u> limit the Power-of-Attorney clause in some fashion. At the end of this clause I give some acceptable examples).

Artist agrees to perform all engagements and to make all appearances in accordance with all agreements entered into by Manager on Artist's behalf. Manager is not authorized to enter into any agreement, the length of which is longer than 3 (three) months, without consulting with Artist.

(Now this last sentence seems to solve the problem by limiting the power-to-sign to contracts less than 3 months long. Except for one thing - it says they can't do it "...without consulting with Artist". <u>This should be unacceptable</u> from the Artist's point of view! It should state "without Artist's <u>prior written approval</u>"!!! "Consulting" means they just have to <u>talk</u> to the Artist about it - yet they can do what they want, anyway! If it's 3 months - maximum 6 months - or over, they should have to get Artist's prior written approval.

Another way is to just limit Manager's power of signing to "short term engagements", perhaps three one-nighters in a row at a venue.

A 3rd option goes the total opposite direction from the original clause - the Manager can't sign <u>anything</u> without the Artist's prior approval. This is not recommended because the Artist shouldn't want to have to deal with every minor type thing, especially if they're on tour across the world!

9. As compensation for Manager's services herein, Artist agrees to pay Manager a sum equal to twenty (20%) percent of all gross compensation received by Artist, Artist's heirs, administrators, executors or assigns, or by any party on Artist's

behalf, from all sources as the result of Artist's professional activities, …

(There are a variety of ways that Managers may be paid. The main ones are: a fixed rate, a sliding scale, a combination of the two, or as an "Employer".

1. A fixed rate should be no lower than 15% of the gross and no higher than 25% of the gross, where "gross" means "before expenses are taken out".

2. An example of a "sliding scale" would be where Manager maybe receives 15% if Artist makes less than $75,000 that year, 20% if Artist makes $75,001 to $200,000, and 25% if the Artist makes $200,001 and up.

3. A combination of the two could be where the rate is, for example, fixed at 20% for everything except live performances, where a sliding scale is used depending on how much the Artist makes per performance or week.

4. In an Employer/Employee contract, the Artist receives a salary. The Artist must be very careful of this type! Try to avoid it unless it's for 6 months or less; or ends, or is adjusted to one of the above, if there's a Record Deal.

Note: Certain advanced money, that is allocated to advance Artist's career, should not be commissionable. Examples would be money to be used for recording and touring expenses - not touring profits; lighting, opening acts, etc. where the money is an advance or expense to Artist, or has to be paid back to someone advancing it.)

...and from any and all agreements entered into during the term hereof; and including any extensions, renewals or substitutions, and any and all balances of terms of any agreements entered into during the term hereof but extending beyond the Manager's term.

(Beware: this continuation of the clause in simple language means, for example: "If the Artist signed any agreement while signed to this Manager, and this Record Deal, for example, lasts longer than the agreement with the Manager, the Artist may still have to pay Manager's commission on these items even AFTER the Manager's contract is over!!!"

As weird as it sounds, the Artist, in a way, has to think about when the contract is over, even considering hiring the <u>next</u> possible Manager, while they're signing with the 1st Manager! Simply put, the Artist doesn't want to have to pay both Managers!!!

Well, there are 3 ways to try to ease the pain.

1. The Artist stays with their original Manager - one reason why they should choose one Very Carefully!

2. Use a "reverse sliding scale" that goes down, for example, from 20% during the actual contract Term, to 0% by the fifth year afterward. Maybe, Manager would receive 10% in the 1st and 2nd years after contract is over, 5% for the 3rd and 4th years on items signed during the term with them, but extending beyond the term with them.

3. Take out all references to "extensions, renewals or substitutions". But that's not fair to the Manager who worked hard to achieve these signings. It's very

unlikely anyway, that a potential Manager would agree to this.

4, Also, keep in mind it may include Songwriting and other "intellectual property" created *during the Term!* The word "Term", meaning length of time, should be capitalized, while "term" be defined a piece of the Agreement

10. Any and all compensation and expenses referred to herein shall be paid to Manager at the end of each calendar month.

11. Artist and Manager shall keep receipts of all expenses incurred,

(Yes, <u>both</u> should keep any and all receipts.)

and Artist and Manager shall keep complete books and records of all monies received as to which Artist and Manager is accountable to the other hereunder.

(Yes, both should keep books and records.)

Artist shall have the right to inspect and examine Manager's said books and records at Manager's business offices during normal business hours within fifteen (15) days upon notice to Manager by Artist, and Manager shall similarly have the right to inspect and examine Artist's said books and records (including those of any corporation or third party receiving monies in her behalf **(see next clause)**) at the place at which the same are kept or maintained within fifteen (15) days' notice and during normal business hours. Any inspection of books and records of Artist or Manager shall not occur more than four times a calendar year.

(Why only 4 times a year? If Manager doesn't limit the amount of times, Artist might show up every day as a kind of harassment, if they want to get out of the contract. Artists

receive their big monies quarterly or semi-annually, anyway.)

12. Manager shall collect and receive all gross compensation payable to Artist under all contracts for the employment of Artist's services and work products that are made and entered into during the term of Manager's service for Artist in the Agreement; and Artist hereby authorizes and appoints Manager as her special agent for collection and attorney-in-fact to collect and receive all such monies in cash and by check, and to give receipts therefore and endorse Artist's name on any such checks and deposit all such receipts in a separate account.

(As in the Power-of-Attorney clause -#8- Manager is granted the right to sign the Artist's name to checks and receipts! The Artist might not want Manager to have this power. At the same time, the Manager might not want Artist handling the money.

A "mutually agreed-upon 3rd party" (a Money Manager that both the Manager and Artist can agree to), may solve this problem. This person, acting as a Business Manager, would handle all the money situations. Now normally, the Personal Manager initially handles the money until the Artist is making so much that it becomes too time consuming and beyond the ability of a Personal Manager to handle the responsibility. But, the Artist can use one from the beginning, understanding that it will cost them a few percent.)

Manager agrees not to co-mingle Artist's funds with any other monies.

(Whoever handles the money should keep Artist's money in a separate account - without *anybody* else's money mixed in!)

13. Manager will send all accounting statements, payments and notices under this Agreement to Artist at her address stated above or to such other address as she may give Manager from time to time hereafter. All notices, accounting statements and payments that Artist is required or desires to give Manager hereunder shall be sent to Manager's address as stated above, or to such other address as he may notify Artist of from time to time hereafter.

(This clause just states what addresses Manager and Artist will send anything regarding the other. Manager and Artist should always keep each other up to date regarding present applicable addresses, email addresses, and phone numbers.)

14. Artist further covenants and agrees that she will faithfully and conscientiously and to the best of her ability, give such auditions and submit to such tests as will from time to time be arranged for Artist by Manager, using such material in connection therewith as Manager may direct Artist to use.

(Here it states that Artist will perform whenever and wherever using whatever material Manager wants, even if it is nonpaying, such as a promotional gig. Regarding song material, I personally would never have an Artist do a song they can't stand due to the fact it would be hard for them to "feel" and put across. A compromise song might work instead.)

And where engagements are obtained for Artist with respect to her activities hereunder, she will fulfill and perform such engagements to the very best of her ability.

(An Artist should <u>always</u> perform to the best of their ability no matter what! It should become a habit!)

15. Artist hereby specifically authorizes and empowers Manager, whenever the Manager may deem the same necessary in

order to further promote and advance Artist's career hereunder, to employ the services of a booking agent or agents for such purpose, and Artist agrees to pay for such services of such booking agent as aforesaid.

(This just gives power to Manager to hire an Agent at any time, and that the Artist is responsible for paying for the service.)

16. It is understood and agreed that expenses for promotion, publicity and related expenses shall be expended by mutual agreement between the Artist and the Manager, and the cost thereof shall be paid by Artist.

(Many Managers want to be able to spend money when necessary without waiting for the Artist's "OK". A compromise would be that Manager could not spend over, say, $500 at any one time, or more than $2,500 in any month, without Artist's prior approval.

It is understood that expenses mentioned herein shall not include Manager's office, legal and accounting expenses or any other costs for doing business.

(Manager should not charge Artist for personal and/or non-related expenses, such as what should be charged to another Artist they represent.)

17. The term of this Agreement shall be for a period of one (1) year from the date hereof with an option to the Manager **(Artist has no choice, the way it's written!)** that this Agreement shall automatically be extended and renewed for an additional period of five (5) years unless Manager cancels this Agreement by notice to Artist in writing thirty (30) days prior to expiration of the original term hereof.

(According to this contract, Manager may keep Artist for 6 years. (By the way, if there's no stated complete length of time listed - it's for <u>life</u>!)

Now what if the Manager isn't doing their job, competently and/or to the best of their ability? Would the Artist want to waste away possibly 6 very important years of their career?

A definite: <u>any</u> time, in <u>any</u> contract, a length of time is involved, unless it's under, say, 3 months, there should be a means of "Escape" if the other party isn't doing their job. An "Escape Clause", sometimes called a "Release Clause" must be added. This provides that:

1. If a <u>specific</u> goal is not being reached... (such as "a Recording Contract with a Nationally Recognized and distributed Major Label", or 500,000 Streams, or... etc.) ...

2. ...in a <u>specific</u> period of time... (Such as, 18 months) then,

3. ...the Artist may request release from the contract.

This guarantees that the Manager must cause some real accomplishment(s) for the Artist - or the Artist can leave the contract if the goals are not reached, and you can get out of a bad situation!

You will find a sample "Rider" with an Escape Clause at the end of Part 1 of this Agreement, written as a "Rider".

18. It is further understood and agreed that any termination of this Agreement shall not relieve Artist of her obligation to reimburse Manager for costs and expenses previously incurred by

Manager in performing services for Artist under this Agreement and any and all unpaid loans and advances that Manager previously made to Artist under this or any other Agreement between Artist and Manager shall immediately become due and payable upon the date of such termination; and Artist agrees to discharge all of her said obligations to Manager within ninety (90) days of termination of this Agreement.

Simply put, Artist is to repay any moneys put out by Manager within 90 days of the end of the contract – but make sure it's not what could be considered an "Investor" type situation regarding your career.

19. If Artist believes Manager has violated this Agreement, or has failed to perform the terms hereof, and this violation or failure to perform is believed to be a significant violation of this Agreement, it shall not be considered a true significant violation of this Agreement if within twenty (20) days after Artist acquires knowledge of such violation or failure to perform, Artist serves written notice on Manager by certified mail of such violation or failure to perform, and Manager cures the same within a further period of forty-five (45) days after receipt of such notice from Artist. The same provisions for notice of violation of contract and time for cure shall also be afforded to Artist.

(This clause, as written, states that, if Artist believes that Manager has violated their Agreement in some important manner, Artist has to notify the Manager within 20 days of when he/she finds out about this problem, and Manager has 45 days to "solve" the problem. As Artist I would recommend that "time for cure" be reduced to 15 to 30 days, if at all possible.

The Artist is also given the same rights if Manager believes the Artist has violated the Agreement in some major fashion.

20. No waiver by Manager of any breach or any covenant or provision of this Agreement shall be deemed to be a waiver of any preceding or succeeding breach of the same or any other covenant or provision.

(First of all, if I was the Artist, I would want it to say: "No waiver by Artist or Manager...". What the clause is saying is that, using an example, "If I let you slide this time by not taking my commission from this particular gig, it doesn't mean that you still don't owe me for the last gig you owe me for, or that I'll let you ignore it the next time!"

It's like an exemption, from a clause, this time, but this is an exception from the rule. And don't expect me to ignore it next time.

21. In the event of any dispute under or relating to this Agreement, the same must be submitted to arbitration to the American Arbitration Association in __**(Name of city)__, ___(Name of State or Commonwealth)_____**, in accordance with the rules promulgated by the said association, and judgment upon the award entered by the arbitrators may be entered into any court having jurisdiction thereof. The award of the arbitrators shall be final and binding on all parties hereto. In the event of arbitration, the prevailing parties shall be entitled to recover any and all reasonable attorney's fees and other costs incurred therein as may be awarded by the arbitrators.

(Why is this clause in there? If you ever want to sue someone, court cases can take years! If you use the American Arbitration Association, it can be solved in months! The Artist and Manager would agree on a lawyer or three (preferably well "versed" in the Music Biz) to act as Judge. The "judge's" ruling can be taken by the winning party to a real Judge, and that Judge will sign off on it, usually without question, and makes the ruling by the lawyer stand up as if tried in a normal court of law.)

22. Should any provision of this Agreement be void or unenforceable, such provisions shall be deemed modified or omitted to the extent necessary to achieve validity or enforceability, and this Agreement, with such provisions so modified or omitted, shall remain in full force and effect.

(This clause says that, if there ever is a problem with any part of the actual contract, any changes and deletions that are used to solve the problem, along with the non-affected contract clauses, will still be in force.)

23. This Agreement may not be modified except by an instrument in writing, and this Agreement shall be construed in accordance with the laws of the **(State)** or **(Commonwealth)** of __(Name)__.

(In the beginning of Paragraph 23, it should state that "…this is the entire agreement between the parties…", meaning only what's in the written agreement, counts. It's a legal necessity.)

24. This Agreement may not be assigned by Manager without Artist's prior approval.

(One little sentence can be so dangerous! In a good deal of contracts, the clause says:

"This Agreement may be assigned by Manager"**.

What that means is, the Manager who the Artist has chosen to guide their career, may sell, give away, swap, whatever, Artist's contract, or any piece of it to someone else - and the Artist could end up possibly with some stranger as their new Manager!**

Clause should state: "This Agreement may **not** be assigned by Manager" or "This Agreement may **not** be assigned by Manager without Artist's prior written approval."

Another thing the Artist can do, or should do if the Artist is signed to a Management Company, and there's more than one Manager in the company, Artist can request a "Key-Person clause", which means that the person of Artist's choice, will remain the key-person in charge of Artist's day-to-day career - or the Artist may ask to be released from the contract)

25. Artist warrants and represents that Artist has been advised of Artist's legal right to seek legal counsel of Artist's own choosing in connection with the negotiation of this Agreement. Artist acknowledges that Manager has advised Artist, and given Artist the opportunity, to seek the advice of independent counsel, and Artist acknowledges that Artist is executing this Agreement voluntarily after consultation with independent counsel, or after Artist's informed decision not to seek the advice of independent counsel.

(Simply put: This contract is very important to both the Artist and the Manager - both sides should have competent legal help - with someone who really knows the Music Biz, and how it operates!)

In witness whereof, the parties hereto have signed this Agreement the day and year specified below, which shall be the effective date of the Agreement.

_____ L. S. **(L. S. = "Legal Signature")**
Artist

Address: _____

Soc. Sec. No _____. Date: _____

_____ L. S. Date: _____
Manager

Address: _____

Remember, if there is more than one person listed in first Paragraph under "hereinafter referred to as Artist", **there should be L. S., Date, Address and Social Security spaces for** <u>each</u> <u>individual</u> <u>person</u>.

And, if there is more than one person signing as the Artist, there needs to be a "Group Supplement" where each band member is tied together to the others, through their name and otherwise, and includes what they can do and can't do, what happens when someone leaves, etc., etc.

<u>**Important Notes**</u>

You should check into having your contract "Notarized" in the locality initially named at the beginning of this Agreement or have Witnesses sign the Agreement.

Nowadays you can get papers "digitally signed," but I prefer, someone prints it out, signs it, and scans it back in and sends it to the other "party."

Make sure there are no blank spaces where info can be filled in, and I recommend everyone initial every page.

If it ever becomes necessary to ink in some changes, that's fine, as long as where every inserted change, both sides should initial it in ink.

If Artist(s) is under 18, there must be a "Guardian Clause", where a parent or guardian must sign the contract promising that the Artist will honor the contract – even after they reach legal age.

All pages should be numbered as such: "Page 1 of 5" (where there are 5 total pages) "Page 2 of 5", etc.

R I D E R

(A "Rider" is an attachment that sometimes appears at the back of an Agreement on a separate sheet of paper which is there to make a particular exception(s) to what was written in the main part. I've given some examples:)

TO: Management Agreement between ____**(Name)**__ (called Manager); and _____**(Name)**_____ (called Artist) Dated: __/__/_

----

1. (a) NOTWITHSTANDING any other provision of this Agreement, in the event that Manager is unable to produce or cause to be produced a legitimate Recording Contract for Artist, on or before the expiration of eighteen (18) months from the date listed below, Artist shall have the right to terminate this Agreement by giving Manager written notice of such termination within 30 days following the expiration of said period.

(This is a form of "Escape Clause" mentioned earlier: #1a allows Artist to leave in 18 months if Manager did not achieve a predetermined goal. This is much better than 6 years!

But, there is a Major Problem with the Way it's Written, above. It says Manager only has to get Artist a "legitimate" recording contract. Manager could start his/her own company (and also sign Artist to it if he/she has an unlimited Power-of-Attorney Clause! See Clause #8).

An "Escape Clause" should have a more specific goal. For example – if you want to go with a Major: "a legitimate recording contract with a nationally recognized and distributed Major Label".

Also, the goal can be anything the Artist and Manager agree upon. It could be to make a certain amount of money within a specified time, such as $200,000 by the end of the 2nd year. And/or You would have 500,000 Streams, and/or so many "Features" – guest appearances on other recordings. And/or the Manager might have to place 3 songs Artist has written within a specified time with a nationally recognized and distributed Major Label or subsidiary Artist, as examples.)

(b) In the event that Artist enters into an agreement within twelve (12) months of the expiration of said 18 months, with any company to which Manager had represented Artist, then Manager shall be deemed to have obtained said agreement and Artist shall not have the right to terminate this Agreement as provided herein.

(This clause protects Manager if Artist delays or turns down interest from a particular company that Manager had approached, then waits until contract is over, and then goes him/herself directly to that same company! That is why the next line, (c), is also added…)

(c) Artist shall not unreasonably withhold approval of any such agreement.

L. S. _____ Date: _____

L. S_____ Date: _____

Section 3:

The Manager Looks for an Artist

("You" Are, Or Want to Be, a "Manager")

1. Why Become a Manager?

A. You love Music, but you feel you're better suited to, or more interested in, the business side of music.

B. You feel you have the capability to be a great Manager.

C. You've found an Artist you believe is outstanding and you feel you could do a great job of managing him/her/ them.

2. When **Not** to Become a Manager

A. Someone, "pulls you into it;" it's not your idea and you're really not into it.

B. You don't have the time, energy and/or income to give your all.

3. Important Qualities of a **Great** Manager

A. They have a lot of Experience in the Music Business - the one thing that can't be taught. There's nothing like actually experiencing the "ins and outs" of the biz - that is, actually doing it - experiencing it!

B. They have great knowledge of the Music Biz, and knows how the Music Biz really operates.

C. They have a great knowledge of Managing. They know what to do, and when to do it, with their particular Artist.

D. They have Great Contacts.

    1. The Manager knows "the right people" in the Entertainment Business, and they know who to go to get everything taken care of that they can't.

    2. The right Entertainment People in the Biz know the Manager (and respect him/her!).

E. They're Persistent.

    1. They never give up, realizing it only takes one "Yes!" out of 100 or more "No's!" to become successful, or at least on the road to success.

    2. They know that a persistent Manager has a better chance of being in the right place at the right time!

F. Although they'd prefer to have everything done "yesterday", they have Patience - they realize it does take some time to get to the end wished-for result.

G. They have a great business mind.

H. They're Street-wise - He's/she's a great "wheeler-dealer".

I. They have the ability to get along with all kinds of people.

J. They have a positive outlook on life in the Biz - they *know* they can get the job done - they believe in themselves and their Artist(s).

K. They're Honest!

L. They're Tactful - they know how to get their point across without offending anyone.

M. They're Creative - They know what it takes creatively - music-wise and business-wise - and know how to attain the results they want.

N. They recognize a great, marketable Artist or Song when they see and hear them!

4. The Main Two Options of Employment for a Manager:

A. Being with an established Management Company.

1. Experienced Companies have experience, cash flow, office facilities, phones, people and business and other contacts. In this case, you, as a potential Manager:

a. You will learn and understand the ins and outs of working with Artists, without risking your last penny in learning!

b. You will realize and understand the problems and learn how to solve them.

c. You can bring along your own Artist to Manage and possibly work out a deal with them. For example, you could split the management percentage with them (Co-Managing).

d. Benefit from merely being associated with them.

(1). It will help your prestige - that is, it will help build your own name in management.

(2). You will have an edge in approaching other Artists as a potential Manager.

As the current state of the Music Business is becoming more and more "up in the air", especially with the economy and digital revolution leaving everyone scared and confused, many Major Record Labels and their Subsidiaries will now only open up their pocketbooks if the Artist is managed or co-managed by an experienced and known Manager or Management Company.

Therefore, I recommend you at least start out with, and remain friends with a well-known Management Company; or Co-manage the Artist (share management) with a known Manager/Management Company.

You *can* start off on your own ...

    B. Doing it on one's own. In this case the Manager will need:

        1. Money for, in part:

           a. Phone bills

           b. Postage and mailings

           c. A Computer. With computers a person can save a lot of money in the long run by doing their own, (for example):

               (1). Business records

               (2). Promotional items for yourself and your Artist

               (3). Promotion using the Internet, especially Social Media (Necessary!)

           d. Lawyer's fees

           e. Accountant's fees

           f. Traveling expenses

g. Sometimes to speed up the process you'll pay for Artist's things, such as:

    (1). Recordings (if not available)

    (2). Photographs

    (3). Web Site

    (4). Traveling, equipment rental and other related expenses.

h. An office, if you can afford to, and don't want to work out of your house; though in the beginning, your house will do nicely, if it's comfortable and has a good "atmosphere" to conduct business.

i. Surviving, until you can earn money from managing.

2. Energy - and lots of it! To become a successful Manager one needs energy. A Manager must "move" even when standing or sitting still.

3. Plenty of persistence - continually planning, pushing, striving, & looking for opportunities. Every minute of the business day (however long), a successful Manager is…

    a. Making contacts

    b. "Selling" themselves

    c. "Selling" their Artists

4. More than one Artist! Don't rely on one Artist for your income, no matter how great they're admired. Anything can happen. Things change for any number of reasons.

5. A great Entertainment Attorney. One who can, and will...

a. Inform you about laws in the state that may affect your business, and yourself.

b. Be extremely helpful to your career in contractual dealings with people and companies.

c. Give you "the experience" you need.

Above I stated that successful Managers have "lots of experience". Well, no one can start out with lots of experience. But, you can align yourself with someone who has that experience - and Name to give you some needed Power! A respected entertainment attorney is one option!

d. Have other clients who can help you

e. Help you financially...

(1). By working on a percentage of a deal, rather than insisting all on cash in advance; some will - but it's becoming rarer every day.

(2). May be able to find investors/financial backing...

(a). ... to form a "Management Company".

(b). ... to back an Artist. (In this case, the backer and the Artist can become partners, without Manager having to split the management income).

(c). No matter how you do it, always have an attorney draw up an agreement that is fair for everyone involved.

No matter how much money a Manager begins with, or whose money it is, if everything is going out and nothing is coming in, the Manager is in trouble!

  C. Other options in Management

    1. Become an "Associate Manager". This means working as an equal partner <u>with</u> another Manager or Management Company regarding a particular Artist.

    2. Become an "Assistant Manager". This means working <u>for</u> another Manager regarding a particular Artist.

    3. Become a Management Consultant. This means working as a consultant to others regarding one or more of their Artists. (Obviously, you don't start out here! The author does this)

    4. Career Guidance. Help a Manager or Artist on an hourly, monthly or yearly basis, helping guide their career or project(s). (Obviously, you don't start out here, either! The author does this, also)

<u>Note:</u> *Yes, I handle numbers 3 & 4 above helping Artists and their Managers, but I have 35 years' experience in the Music Biz and Music Biz Contractual side, plus a lifetime on the Creative side. And I always have to be up to date on all that's happening in the Music Industry.*

5. Choosing an Artist to Manage

  A. You must be extremely picky in selecting Artists to Manage. As I stated before, the Artist should choose a Manager very carefully. It applies equally to a Manager choosing an Artist. A Manager is putting their...

1. ... time on the line: you will be spending time, on the project. Make sure the Artist is worth your time and energy.

2. ... money on the line: you will be spending money, just existing, yourself, while you're working on the project. Your office expenses are continuing no matter what, so why not expend them, as well as your time, on projects of maximum potential?

3. ... Name/Reputation on the line: Your Name Is On The Line! Handing in a great project will enhance your name. Handing in a less-than-great project may harm your name, and therefore, your career!

B. Simply put:

Is the Artist So Creative, and So Marketable, that you'd be Really Stupid if you Didn't Manage them?!

When considering whether you should become involved in Managing a particular Artist, ask yourself the following questions:

1. Do they have **DRIVE?!** That is, do they have insatiable ambition? *Passion?* Will they settle only for the top? Are they obsessed with "making it BIG"? Will they not let anything get in their way? Are they Persistent? Do they believe in hard work - on and off stage – and are always giving it all they have?

2. Do they have **MAGIC?!** Do they "glow in the dark"? Do they create electricity all around them - especially on stage? Do they have "sex appeal"? Do they have "charisma"? Do they have "The Look"?

Call it what you want - I call it MAGIC! When you see them, are you and others "glued to them" - and they won't let you go? Are people hypnotized? (<u>Note:</u> It's got to be there naturally - it's not an act.)

3. Are they **Great ENTERTAINERS** - Not just simply Singers or Musicians?! Do they have Style? Do they have Great Showmanship? Are they *ALIVE*? Do they Enjoy Entertaining? Does their performance come from their *Heart* - not their head? Are they having Fun? Do they still have that "little kid" in them?

4. Do they have **Great SONGS?!** Do their Songs hypnotize you and take you to another world? Do you find yourself still "hearing them" even after you're finished listening – that is, they *stay with you*. (Unless you can get great Songs elsewhere that fit them.)

5. Are they **UNIQUE?!** Do they Stand Out from the crowd - and other Artists? Do they have their own "sound", their own "Image"?

BUT, they still must be **MARKETABLE**! That is, many people will want to see them and buy their product!)

6. Do they have **Loads** of **CONFIDENCE?!** Do they believe in themselves so much that they are not afraid to let down all their "walls" and allow themselves to be vulnerable and sensitive to their audience? Do they have a "fear of success", where they put roadblocks in their own path?

7. Do they know, and accept, that the **MUSIC BUSINESS** is a **BUSINESS?!**

8. Do they treat their Fans like Family? Through Social Media & otherwise?

An Artist that passes all these tests is a very special person or Group of people. You may see or hear hundreds of acts before you find that someone "Special."

C. If you think you've found what you've been looking for...

Become thoroughly familiar with the Performer(s) both on and offstage. Take the time to...

1. Carefully observe them under all situations.

2. Evaluate them making sure they are "the real thing".

3. Don't be paranoid; just be cautious!

Section 4:

Putting the Pieces Together

1. Follow the Leader

From now on in this course, "the Manager", and "the Leader" (of the Group), and the Artist are interchangeable, being responsible for the same things affecting the Artist. When a Manager is "hired", he/she takes over a lot, but not all of the responsibilities that the Leader has.

It's the Manager's job also to make sure the Leader is doing their job!

Future Managers: this Section is very important, for you are the "Chief Leader", and the following will really affect the potential success of "the Project"!

Also, if you are a single-person Artist, you may think: "Wait a minute! I just want to go out there and be a Recording Star - I don't want to be part of a Band!" Well, you can start out with that thought in mind, but sooner or later you will want, or need, or have to deal with back-up Musicians, singers, or dancers, or need to form a working Group or Band - or your Record Company will insist on it! No matter what, trust me - the following information is important to know, whether you're working alone or not!

Also keep in mind, nowadays, that live performances are making up more and more of the Artist's income. And you're going to need "side-people," especially in the larger venues!

A. Some people don't want to, or can't be "Leaders". For some, it's necessary or obvious that they should be the Leaders. Singers and Musicians must decide whether to:

1. Join an existing Group or newly forming Group.

2. Form their own Band as its "Leader" or "Spokesperson".

3. Hire Musicians and others when and as needed

B. Being the Leader of a Band may seem neat, but not everyone can do it.

1. It involves a lot more than taking the credit.

2. Many more hours may be spent on business details besides actually leading the Band and playing Music.

3. Their ability at handling the position can often make the difference between success and failure, no matter how great the Band performs.

C. Why must there be a Leader?

1. A pure "Democracy" rarely works in a musical Group. The main business of the Band, playing Music, is not accomplished. Too much time is wasted because:

a. Common agreement is usually hard to reach.

b. Important decisions are left unmade.

c. Trivial things become too important, irritations arise, and bad feelings erupt.

D. Now, it shouldn't be a "Dictatorship". It just means that: The Leader has the controlling vote, and the veto. He/she:

1. Keeps the Band moving musically and career-wise.

2. Pulls people together tactfully.

3. Soothes ruffled feathers.

E. Among the things the Leader is responsible for are:

The key word is "responsible". The Leader is not expected to do everything - they may have help - but they are responsible for these things being done.

1. Setting the Band's goals and the timetable for achieving them.

2. Scheduling and running rehearsals.

3. Choosing the Music the Band will play.

4. Promotion and publicity, including using the different Web Sites - your own & others, including the "social networks" such as Instagram, Twitter, and Face Book, etc.

Note: If there are 5 Band Members, they all should help with the Promotion!

5. Contracting for performances.

6. Making contacts and representing the Group in business.

7. Collecting money for performances.

8. Keeping the books and paying the Band members.

9. Acting as arbitrator in solving personal conflicts and keeping peace in the Group.

F. The Leader/Manager is the one all Band members look to whenever any kind of problem arises.

1. This person must be strong and resourceful in order to handle it.

2. Some people are natural Leaders, and some are not.

3. Only the individual knows, and the Artist cannot afford to be misled by his or her own ego in regard to being the spokesperson.

Being a spokesperson involves being responsible for everything a Manager would do until one is needed and hired. Even after a Manager is hired, the Group still needs one to represent the Group to the Manager and others and to continue handling certain responsibilities.

G. Great Leaders:

1. Know they are part of the team.

2. Keep an open mind about suggestions.

3. Don't allow themselves to feel more important than anyone else.

4. Always make fellow Band members feel equally important.

5. Realize they can't, and shouldn't do everything themselves, so:

a. They discuss with, and delegate tasks and responsibilities to members of the Band.

b. They assign reasonable dates for their completion.

c. They always assign tasks to persons they feel capable of handling them.

d. They coordinate activities handled by different people.

Important note: *Problems within the Band (or any of your team) must be handled immediately! You must prevent them from growing worse. Creative imaginations can work negatively as well as positively, so all Band members should be encouraged to speak out about problems as soon as they arise before they grow into insurmountable obstacles. Always keep all lines of communication open!*

H. When there's a problem:

1. Define it.

2. Put it into words; get it out into the open.

3. Make sure everyone understands what the problem is.

4. Solve it jointly.

5. Make sure your decision is great for the Group - not just you.

2. Starting Out

If you've decided to put together a Duo, Trio, Group, or Band, as in any other business, starting small, keeping expenses down, and concentrating on producing a great product may be the way to go. Very few large businesses start out large, but grow in proportion to their success. You can grow, too, but give yourself a great start first.

A. You might start small...

1. You can add Singers and Musicians later on, when you find the right people.

If you're looking for real "Pros" <u>before</u> you get a record deal, you're gonna need a lot of luck and persistence. The top pros usually come out of the woodwork <u>after</u> you get a deal. That does not mean there aren't great side-people out there that may be interested in joining forces with you!

2. You may not yet have found the right Musicians to build with.

3. Perhaps you prefer to get "tight" with the ones you have. A full Band isn't necessary to be a Performer or recording Artist.

4. You can make out very well as a Singer, Singer/Songwriter, or as part of a Duo or Trio.

5. If you're interested in lighter Music such as Pop, Show Tunes, Light Jazz, Folk, Blues or Country, this might be the right direction for you.

6. It often makes sense for a potential Recording Artist to make the initial demo using just themselves and computerized instrumentation, if necessary, so they can develop their "own sound".

B. Advantages to being "Fewer Than a Full Band."

1. Smaller number of personalities to deal with.

2. Less equipment to lug around and worry about.

a. Usually clubs who hire Singer/Musicians have their own PA sound systems.

b. Renting or buying one will cost far less than the equipment needed for a full Band.

3. You might find a gig where you can play one place for a period of time; sometimes year-round. If you like an ever-changing crowd, as in a hotel, you might find it more interesting than a place with "regulars".

C. A Singer minus instrumental (including digital) accompaniment has narrow choices.

    1. Singing Folk Music or doing "Spoken Word".

    2. Joining a choir, chorus or a theater group

    3. Leading sing-a-longs.

    4. Karaoke

D. Playing an instrument and accompanying yourself expands the number of places to play.

    1. You can team up with a Guitarist or Keyboard Player.

    2. Some singers pick up "Side-men" as needed, sometimes providing sheet Music for Musicians to use for a particular gig.

    3. You may be part of a Duo at one place, and of a Trio or more at another.

    4. Some singers have an Arranger-Conductor who is responsible for hiring Musicians in each town they'll be playing. This keeps expenses small and limits road details.

        a. He/she provides them with sheet Music

        b. He/she rehearses them.

c. Sometimes a core Group, usually a basic rhythm section consisting of keyboard/guitarist, bassist and drummer, travels with the Singer, and other local Musicians are hired as needed.

If you are a Musician, this arrangement provides yet another opportunity for you. It helps to read Music and sometimes it pays to belong to the Musician's union. You'd contact local concert Managers, Promoters and Booking Agents, as well as operators of theaters and supper-clubs, etc., who might book traveling Performers. Let your fellow Musicians know you are available. Your union local will often be able to help you, also.

5. Keyboard Players:

a. Can often find work in restaurants, bars, lounges and clubs, usually of a fairly steady nature. (Guitarists and other Musicians may also, but not as often.)

b. Keyboard players who can sing make out the best.

6. MIDI/Computerized Instruments makes it possible to go out alone or have one Keyboardist, and yet sound like a complete Band. "Looper Pedals" are also being used more & more where one person can provide multiple instruments, by looping what they're playing.

E. You have to get out and hustle, and use the Internet, meeting as many potential employers as possible, and selling yourself or Artist and their ability.

F. Exposure, being seen and heard, is the most important thing.

1. Don't hold out for the "perfect job".

2. Get started somewhere!

3. You *can* move up, if you...

    a. Are *Driven* to succeed.

    b. Continue making contacts.

    c. Constantly improve.

You ever notice how often the Major Artists and Bands show up and play at a small club before going out on tour with their big show so they can get their show "tight". If they can do it, so can you!

3. Expanding - Choosing the Right People for a Group or Band:

Again, remember that the really top pros only become involved after the Artist "makes it" or if the Artist has a great reputation, or they just plain believe in you. But they're not going to stick around unless things start to happen fast...

A. Start thinking about great Musicians, Singers or whomever you may know. If you don't have such contacts, or the people you'd like to have are otherwise occupied, start scouting around.

    1. Put the word out on the street with your friends.

    2. Put an "ad" in the paper, stating what you are doing, and what instruments you need. Aim for papers that have special sections for Musicians, like a "Musician's Grapevine".

    3. Don't forget the Internet, putting the word out on your Web Site and others, and sending out Bulletins through your mailing list and your Instagram/Face Book/Twitter type sites.

4. Visit Music Schools and Colleges and put up flyers and talk to their (music) teachers.

5. Check with Recording Studios - many good Musicians sign up with them to do "session work".

6. Check Music Clubs.

7. Go to "open-mic nights".

8. Check if there are any "Musician referral" type services in your area.

Remember that the focus should be a group designed to play the kind of Music the Artist wants to play and please the audience the Artist plays for.

B. Choosing members must be done very carefully, as though you were choosing members of a closely-knit family. If not chosen carefully there will be delays reaching your creative goals which will take the enjoyment out of your "work". All members should be mutually supportive of each other and the Group as a whole. These Members:

1. Will spend lots of time together in all kinds of situations.

2. Must be comfortable together so they can spend their time making Music rather than arguing and settling disputes.

3. Must be able to depend on each other.

C. When considering hiring a Singer or Musician, take your time about it. Talk with them, draw them out and see how they feel about things in general and the Music business in particular. You'll be able to sense from their attitude what their attitude toward work will be if you choose your questions and topics of conversation, well.

1. Do they have easy, like-able personalities, with a quality of humor as well as seriousness toward their Music?

2. Do they have inflated egos - deadly in a Group - that can destroy the ability to function as a team?

3. Are they willing to do what's best for the Group?

4. Will they accept someone's Leadership?

5. Do they have great attitudes?

6. Do they have the same musical goals you do?

7. Are they willing to proceed step by step toward achieving these goals?

8. Do they possess adequate equipment?

9. Do they have adequate personal transportation?

10. What kind of experience do they have?

No matter how appealing, talented, or even charismatic a Musician may be, if they're going to present a bunch of drama and other problems, your progress will be held up and your Group will not be a happy one.

D. Two major things to watch out for:

1. Addiction to Drugs (including alcohol).

2. Laziness. For example, not liking to practice as often as the group feels necessary.

E. Successful teamwork is achieved only without "stars" who:

1. Overplay,

2. Compete in volume, and/or

3. Exercise their egos.

   a. They shouldn't destroy the Group's effect and ability to put the Songs across to the audience.

   b. The audience is paying to hear what they want to hear. If they don't like what they hear, they won't be there the next time. And neither will you or your Group!

F. If you have potential members of the Band that also happen to be friends and/or relatives, state this to them from the start, something like:

"Please remember and understand that musically we are engaged in a business, and the music comes before anything else when we are working on our careers. You will be treated as any other person in this Group."

1. Yes, a friend or relative may possess an outstanding talent, and deserves a chance. But, consider the effect upon the rest of the Group.

2. You must be willing to fire them as you would anyone else - let them know it before you start. Emphasize that yours is a Group effort - what's best for the Group must be your first consideration.

3. Friends and relatives must be able to "switch hats". In other words, the person must be able to differentiate

between "friend time" and "Music Time", and know that one position can't, and shouldn't affect the other.

G. Musically auditioning potential members:

1. Are they musically competent and able to play in a Group setting? You should listen to them alone and as the play within the Group.

2. You have to watch them *perform* not just play - are they *alive?!*

3. Do you feel they put themselves into their work & fit in? Let the other Members help you decide.

4. Do their particular styles match with the other Members and your "sound"?

4. Choosing your Material

Important: It's obvious that different people have different career goals regarding their Music. But,

1. No matter what style of Music you or your Artist is playing: Rock, Hip Hop, R&B, the Blues, Pop, Jazz, Country, or whatever...

2. Whether you're a solo Artist or a Band or Group...

3. Whether you're doing "O. P.'s" (**o**ther **p**eople's - "covers"), originals, or both...

4. Whether the Songs are old or new...

...the Songs still have to fit certain "patterns"!

A. Each of the following 5 points are very important no matter what direction you choose to follow. When choosing the Songs to represent you or your Artist...

1. They must be "*GREAT Songs*".

2. They must fit your "image".

(Your image is, simply: The Music you play, the way you play it, the way you come across to your audience, and the way you look and act, in public and off stage.)

3. They must be comfortable for you to play.

4. They must be Songs that you as well as the audience can identify with and enjoy.

5. They must be Songs that will cause people in the business to want to employ you because you play them.

B. In regard to the five points above (before I separate playing "Originals" and doing "Cover Songs")...

1. If you don't like a song, and can't picture doing it, don't do it!

a. Write/find Songs you like that fit you and your style, or arrange the Songs so that they do. (Great Songs can be arranged to fit any style. You've heard different versions of the same Song before.)

b. You can't achieve a great performance with any Song you don't like, and it will show.

2. Maybe you haven't come to understand exactly what it is you want to do and therefore choose bad Songs for you.

3. If you find "no market" (no interest) in your choices don't give up:

    a. Try a little different direction.

    b. Rethink the whole situation through and make the changes that feel right.

It's taken some Musicians a number of false starts before they found their groove. Flexibility is the keynote! Also realize that, your favorite type of Music may not be who you "really are"!!!

4. The area in which you're located often makes a difference.

    a. "Thrash Metal" may not be big in Nashville, for instance, but Country is.

        (i). If you can't make a living where you are doing the Music that you like best - think about going to where it sells. Now, I don't recommend you just up and move there until you check it out first. The area may not be the way you imagined! Do a "business vacation" there for a week or two, first and thoroughly check out the scene)

        (ii). You should be able to get a good idea of the scene through your Internet "Social Networks".

C. Choosing the right Original Songs:

1. Obviously something you'll have to be *great* at if you want a successful performing and recording situation.

2. The challenge is finding Songs the Record Companies want to record, unless you want to put out your songs on your Own Record Label, (which is a good way to start,

nowadays, anyway.) It *does* have to be "Marketable", no matter which direction you wish to go.

3. Don't restrict your efforts to just your own original material.

    a. Be open-minded; be willing to co-write and/or look to writers even outside the Band, always looking to material that fits the requirements of the companies.

Important Note: *If you wish to go with a Major Label or large Indie, it's important to be able to get your foot in the door. Give them a little of what they want, and you'll have a better chance of doing more of what You want.*

    b. Pleasantly accept, but don't take to heart, the advice and comments of friends and relatives who are not in the Music business. They are unlikely to be objective.

4. Go out and perform, and show your stuff to Disc Jockeys, Managers, Agents, experienced Studio Musicians, Music Publishers or Record Producers if you can. Listen to them and let them guide you, for they are tuned to what's happening.

5. You never know where great original material will come from. By looking in the right places you will have better odds. Listen to everyone's material.

    a. Managers, Producers, Publishers and Song-agents may have Writers they are trying to hook up with someone who will play *their* material.

    b. Some areas have Songwriter's clubs who have members who are trying to do the same thing as you - have a Hit Record!

c. Go to open-mic nights and listen to songs on the Internet

d. Someone may seek you out.

   (1). Be receptive.

   (2). If their material is great and "commercially viable", and you believe it can make you a success - do it.

   (3). But make sure you like it and that it fits you, and you fit it.

   D. When you're doing "Covers", but also want to play "Originals"

I've run into many Bands that play cover material under one group name and originals under a different name. Also keep in mind that you can expand venues where you play by performing, as an example, as a duo one place, trio another and a full band at others. You can also play acoustic at some and electric at others.

   1. Many of you would rather be doing originals, but keep in mind that meanwhile...

      a. You need to survive to play another day, not merely to win a meaningless battle by playing only original Songs.

      b. Surviving, paying bills, and saving up to make the recording of your best material, is the way to do it.

   2. There are fewer places that hire Bands who play only originals, but yes, there is a way to play just originals anyplace you want, and earn a good living.

<u>Fact:</u> *The Key to doing what you want corresponds directly to how many people you can pull in to hear you. 98% of the time, the most important thing in the world to the club, restaurant, or other people who may employ you is: MONEY!!! I'm sorry to say, but they don't care <u>what</u> you play - or often, even how good you play it - if you can bring in a ton of people!!!*

If you want to play what you want to play and the way you want to play it, you can take the following steps:

a. Play whatever you have to play to get gigs (but play the material in your style, if possible). Your acceptance will be made easier by playing what club owners and audiences want, and you'll get that important "exposure" faster besides building a "following".

b. Start an e-mail list. Have people who like you give you their name and e-mail address and/or phone number. This will help you to get more gigs. (The bigger the list, the more and better the gigs.)

c. Build up your Internet "Friends" list and "Plays"!

d. Make sure everyone knows <u>your</u> e-mail address, your web site(s), including Instagram/Facebook-type sites. Announce them everyplace you play, up on stage and through stickers, flyers, etc., that you give out at your gigs.

3. Let's say, you have originals you think are winners, and you want people to listen to them:

a. Try playing the "covers" most of the time, and now and then slip in an original without announcing it. Chances are people will be interested in hearing it if they like the other things you're doing even though playing all new material might initially turn them off.

b. If people respond to your originals positively you're on your way; your following continues to build. Without a big following, gigs are few and the money small.

c. Now take this information regarding your "large following" to whoever is in charge of where you want to play. Convince them that these people will show up to see you. Proof can be a videotape you took of the last crowd to see you.

If you follow the above steps, you could be on your way. Yes, it might take a little time. But meanwhile, you've been paying your dues, you've gotten your Songs and show tighter (including your style and image), you're getting better and more gigs, playing what you want to play, and now you're ready for anything!

E. When you're playing "Cover Songs":

1. Try to inject your own style - if you want to stand out. Part of your PR image is the way you arrange Songs to further it.

a. The Song should be recognizable, but your interpretation of it (your arrangement) is a distinct mark of identity.

b. Just because a Song is a hit on a recording it's no reason for you to totally imitate it and doing so will not help you.

Some club owners may insist you play songs close to the original recording.

c. You want to stand out from other Bands in your own style.

2. Yes, gigs come a lot easier playing "Top 40" or other kinds of popular cover Songs. Most people like, and look for, the familiar. They want to hear Music they know and can hum along with. But, if they know and like your originals...

Section 5:

Getting Your Performing Act Together

1. The Art of Successful Practice

Practices are extremely important whether for local or national gigs, or for Recording.

    A. Take charge.

        1. Do everything in an organized manner.

            a. Everyone should know when and where the practice sessions are.

            b. Establish in advance what pieces you'll be doing.

            c. Treat practices like a performance right from the start. Don't be a dictator, but keep everyone on course.

            d. You <u>can</u> have fun <u>and</u> be professional.

                (1). If you treat practices professionally, your Musicians will realize how important they are.

                (2). Solid practices bind a Band or Group together more than even performances.

        2. Keep aware of what is going on:

            a. Look for difficulties members may be having.

            b. The "pressure" of a performance where everything must be right the first time, isn't there. Do it over and over again until it works.

c. Be aware of personal problems between Band members.

   (1). Straighten out the situation immediately.

   (2). You have many responsibilities and no time to waste on side issues.

3. Set goals to achieve and make up schedules to achieve them.

Example: Suppose you're now a duo and looking for a bass player. Assign a date by which you will hopefully have found the right someone and work like hell to make it. This addition may make it possible for you to expand the kind of places you play.

4. Scheduling is important regarding dates for completing Songs.

   a. A certain number of Songs should be learned within a specified period of time. For example: 5 songs per week.

   b. If things progress well, when you see that you're down to the last 5 songs, for example, start looking to play dates soon after they are learned.

5. Practice and work until you feel ready and then go after those play dates (or Recording situation).

   a. Don't "think" you'll be ready by such and such a date, *know* you'll be because you've thought it through and weighed out all the possibilities.

   b. Make changes when necessary, not because of whims.

c. Plan everything you do; carry out those plans and you'll achieve it.

6. During practice there are just as important, if not more important, things to also concentrate on - especially concerning the Artist's image! How Artist/Musicians look, and act is extremely important.

a. Your Artist/Group must look very much *ALIVE!* Not dead!

b. Artist must develop and form a relationship with their audience. (Nowadays, potential fans want to be drawn into the Artist's world – and become a part of it!)

c. Artist must have a great show! This includes Artist(s) appearance and the stage and equipment's appearance, also! It's ENTERTAINMENT"

d. All equipment must be functioning properly - including your lighting equipment!

2. Working Out Your Repertoire

A. You've carefully worked on the music you're going to play. Now: making the Songs come *Alive*.

1. Whatever you have - whether CDs, mp3s, lead-sheets, chord charts, sheet music, or lyric sheets - distribute them!

2. Have the Musicians and Singers get familiar with the material as quickly as possible.

3. The "Key" is important

The Songs must be in the right key for the Singer(s):

a. Determine it through trial and error, if necessary.

b. If anyone is struggling with a part, try shifting to different keys until it's right.

Rule of thumb: The highest note in the Song should be the highest note that an Artist can reach comfortably, sounding great.

4. Arranging your music - the notes & the rhythms you play.

Important: Your "Sound" is what's going to set you apart from every other Artist. Think of your favorite Artist/Superstars - no one sounds like them! They have/had their own individualistic rhythms, chord changes, arrangement style, production style or whatever - that made them sound like Them!

a. You may "fall into it" by playing songs and jamming.

b. You may have a Band member who understands "the sound" you want, and can communicate it to the others.

c. This person should listen to the other Musician's ideas, but if necessary, be able to arrange the material for the Group. If he/she's open minded, agreeable, and a great Arranger, your Group will have the sound you want.

5. If no one inside the Group can handle the arrangements, employ someone from outside - an experienced Arranger.

Regardless of who does the arranging, the leader should maintain "artistic control" so that the Group's individual sound is maintained.

6. Everyone should be given a chance to use and expand his/her talents. Try different people on leads - singing or soloing on an instrument. This:

  a. Makes them feel useful and important.

  b. Gives the regular leads a break.

  c. Gives your sets more variety.

  d. Makes your Group not only appear more versatile and professional, but actually become so.

  e. Gives the leader more strength and respect from the Group.

Always let a Musician, at first, try to feel a part out himself. They might come up with a better "line" than you had thought of. If it works, it works. If what they play doesn't work, then find a part you both agree on.

  B. A newly formed Group will need time to get the first Songs sounding right. The first ones are always the hardest:

  1. You have to get used to each other, working together.

  2. You're not just learning a Song - you're creating your Sound - a main part of your "Image"!

It may seem to be taking longer getting things started than you feel necessary or want it to take. Don't worry. In the beginning things take as long as they need, and agitation over time spent is useless. Try to work efficiently. Do things as often as they need doing and it will work out. Remember - you're trying to come up with a sound that is both unique <u>and</u> marketable, and that may take a little time!!!

3. Suggestions from every member should be listened to and evaluated. If they seem plausible to use, use them!

4. Checking progress is important:

a. The best way (actually, the only way) to do it is by recording your practice sessions.

(1). Listen to the recordings privately, making notes, and play them over a few times before having the Group listen to them.

(2). Don't erase the recordings immediately. You'll want to compare that week's with the next week's, and the next week's, etc.

b. If you do this a few times you'll be better prepared to:

(1). Discuss with the individual Musicians how they sounded.

(2). Comment on the Group's performance as a whole.

c. Some important things to look (out) for are:

(1). The "feel" of the sound.

(2). Is everyone really "putting out"?

(3). How tightly is the Group playing together?

(4). Do variations you have tried come across?

(5). Are certain instruments drowning others?

(6). Is someone playing a "clinker"?

(7). Is the rhythm solid behind the other instruments?

(8). Is everyone on key?

(9). Can you hear the Singer's words?

(10). Is the spirit there?

(11). Are there dynamics? Do the Songs build? (If you start at full force - where do you go from there?!!!)

Practices should be played like performances. If you do this and the recording sounds great, it might help you get a few gigs. If it's really terrific, it could ultimately lead to a Recording Label's interest (along with your Live Performances)!

3. The Mechanics of "Sets"

A. Once the material is learned and everyone is satisfied, organizing the sets is the next step. The order in which the music is placed is very important.

1. Grabbing the audience's attention immediately is the key to a successful start. Holding it will keep the performance successful.

a. Start strong and get stronger, but don't overwhelm the audience and wear them out.

b. A great method is to start strong, end strong, and in the middle ease up a little and make your audience comfortable. That way, whether they realize it or not, they will be waiting for the next set.

2. Too much of the same thing is wearing on an audience as well as the Group.

3. All music is "mood" music in that it influences the listeners. You can effectively "tease" your audience by taking them up and down and spinning them around by the way your music is organized in sets.

B. When you have a set together the way you've decided you'll perform it, record the set.

1. Listen to the playback carefully several times. Your feelings may change about some of the material and/or the order of the songs.

a. A certain Song(s) may not seem to fit.

b. You may have too many fast Songs or too many slow ones.

c. You may have too many sad ones.

d. All the Songs may be too similar in tempo and feeling.

e. The set may feel limp or lifeless. If this happens, the Musicians will react to it, and their performance will be lifeless too.

2. If necessary, make changes, even to learning new material. Don't just "let it go" hoping things will "work out" in performance. Always do whatever is necessary to make your performance as great as possible.

C. Time your sets including the time you might use to talk to your audience.

1. Example: If you're supposed to do a forty-minute set when playing a club or you're an opening act, and you...

    a. Come out considerably less, add a number or two.

    b. If more, cut down.

2. Work this out <u>before</u> you perform so you're never caught having to eliminate one or two of your strongest numbers! Remember- it's very important to start and end *strong*!

D. Keep changing the sets as you acquire and learn more material.

    1. This keeps things interesting both for the audience <u>and</u> the members of the Group.

    2. Playing the same material in the same sequence too many times will guarantee stale performances very quickly. Yes, the audiences like familiar material - but not "sameness"!

4. Sound Check

A. The Sound check is as important as your performance. Before you take the stage for live performances...

    1. Check out the sound equipment and make whatever adjustments are necessary for that room.

    2. Do the sound-check well in advance to allow time for...

        a. Setting up equipment- including "Lights", video,

        b. Making adjustments,

        c. Securing replacements or making repairs.

3. If using rental equipment and a company engineer, or the venue's, they will (should) help.

4. If you're doing it yourself, ask the Manager or owner about the best place to setup.

5. "Feedback" must be avoided - you know, that screeching, honking, or rumbling sound. It occurs when two pieces of equipment are too close together. It may be controlled by...

 a. Moving the mic a couple of inches.

 b. Turning the microphone in another direction.

 c. Lowering the "gain" or volume of the amplifier.

 d. Changing the tone.

 (1). If possible, rearrange the equipment because you may need the volume or tone.

 (2). Keep the microphone from directly facing a speaker while performing.

6. Parametric or Graphic "Equalizers", pieces of equipment that change the frequencies of your output, are important. Every place you play will differ from every other place due to the shape of the place and the materials used for the floors, walls and ceilings.

 a. Experiment, making only slight adjustments until you find out what an equalizer can do, and it sounds right.

 b. Practice with it during your practice sessions.

 c. By changing the frequencies slightly, up or down...

(1). A great deal of feedback can be eliminated.

(2). You can boost tones that appear to be missing.

7. Be sure the volumes and tones of all mics and instruments are adjusted against each other so that you have a great mix of volumes and tones.

Have someone off the stage out in the room listening and checking the sound from various points until an overall great level is achieved. The sound on stage is always set different from the sound in the rest of the room - often by a wide margin (to help prevent feedback)!

a. Take into account what happens when there are people there, with their clothes, hair, etc., absorbing part of the sound.

b. Make sure the instruments don't overpower the Singer or vice versa.

8. Singers must be heard clearly, and the words understood.

a. Musicians should cut down volume a bit when the Singers are singing.

b. "Fills" should be played around the Singers, not over them.

c. When playing a solo, volumes may be turned up, but must be turned back down when the solo is finished.

Many Musicians make the mistake of just turning up their volumes, becoming louder and louder during the course of an evening. This forces the vocalists to be "buried" or to lose their voices trying to compete or just to hear themselves.

        d. Always leave room for adjustments in volume so you have room to build.

    9. Use stage monitors, (speakers on stage), so that Vocalists and Musicians are able to hear themselves.

    By setting the stage monitor's tones lower than the other speakers, the volumes can then be set high enough to be heard clearly, without creating feedback.

    10. Make sure all connections are tight.

        a. Bad or loose connections produce "static", crackling and/or popping noises - or no sound.

        b. Microphones are very sensitive instruments so make sure they are securely plugged in and working.

  B. If you are recording the gig (which you should!)...

    1. Set up the equipment ahead of time.

    2. Record the Band playing through the sound-check.

    3. Make sure everything is operating smoothly before the gig begins.

Helpful hint: Input one channel to your recording deck directly from the mixing board - "direct sound". Then input one channel from a microphone hung in the middle of the room (if possible) for ambient sound - including the audience. This will give you a better "live" sound when mixed together.

4. The "live performance" recording can be tremendously useful in securing bookings.

> a. The "live feeling" is on the recording and the crowd presence is felt as well as their reaction to your playing.

> b. Applause helps! If the reaction is a great one, the element of generated excitement proves you know how to "sell" your music which is important to the music businesspeople who hear it.

C. Video-record your Gig! With video, the combination of sound and visible reaction is even more powerful. You can use it to get gigs - or even a recording contract. (Don't forget to video your audience's enthusiastic reaction!!!)

No matter what, you should video your gigs for other reasons, like to see...

> 1. How your stage performance is coming across. Is it spirited?

> 2. Whether your image is being projected.

> 3. How you and your equipment look - including your Lighting.

> 4. If it's really good, you can put it up on your Social Networking Sites, YouTube and your Web Site, etc., to draw fans to future shows.

If possible, use the sound from your audio recording and sync it up with the video. The sound produced from Video cameras often sounds "bleah."

5. On Stage:

IMPORTANT: The Artist/Group/Band must always do their very best - every Song, every set, every show, and take pride in doing it. Make every show an *Event*! Whether there's a packed house, or only one person out there, it makes no difference. (You never know how "important" or "powerful" that one person might be!) No "We'll sound better the second set!" You are a Professional, an Entertainer, and you should *always* perform like one! It's important to get into the habit of always playing the same way - All Out!

A. You may sometimes feel that getting up there and doing it is the most difficult part of the business. However, you'll find out it's actually much easier than you thought.

1. It's easier by far than all the preparation, practicing and learning you went through to be able to get out there.

Being a little nervous is normal - and actually very good! Nerves are just energy - so put those nerves to work for you!

2. The worst is behind you. All you have to do is...

a. Be yourself,

b. Enjoy yourself, and

c. Make sure the audience has a great time.

B. Start off strong; get their attention, and continue, song, after song, after song!

1. Unless your act involves talking, concentrate on the music.

2. After you have gotten off a few numbers, you might say a few words - and then back to the music.

a. If you use "patter", it has to be great.

b. A little humor never hurts. It shouldn't become the show but merely strengthen it. A few one-liners can make all the difference.

C. Keep your performing tight and professional; don't waste time.

1. Know what song you're going to do next and do it. Make "song lists" of the material and tape them to your instruments if necessary to smooth progressions between numbers. If you have an Engineer and/or "Lighting Person", they should have a list, also.

2. Go out and see well-known and respected Performers. Watch and listen to what they do and observe how smoothly, tightly, and cleanly they do it.

D. Every Song you do should have an exciting ending, one that invites applause. Hearing a strong exciting number and having it end weakly is a tremendous letdown for the audience whether they realize it immediately or not. Popular Groups or Bands perform onstage numbers differently from the endings on their records.

E. The timing of your sets is important.

1. You should be constantly aware of the emotional temperature of the audience. If you've been building the audience to the point where they want a fast, exciting, emotionally explosive Song, playing a slower one is the equivalent of giving them a cold shower. Making changes may be necessary.

a. When you have the "feel" of a particular audience, make changes from the planned order, if necessary, to keep the feeling and the communication.

b. You have to be aware and sensitive to the audience and what they want. Great Musicians are able to cope with this, and with experience welcome it, because it strengthens the relationship with the audience.

F. If people request Songs, don't embarrass them for asking.

1. If you know the Song, want to do it, and it fits into the set, do it.

2. If you don't know the Song, say so and apologize briefly.

3. If you really hate the Song and don't want to perform it, don't do it.

Have Fun! Throw yourself into your performance. There are no strangers or enemies out there, unless you make them that way through your attitude. Be warm and friendly - it pays!

G. People are there to be *Entertained*, and you, the Artist, are there to do it.

1. They're paying for their entertainment.

2. If you make them feel comfortable you've gained a new Group of fans.

3. Make love to them with your eyes, your body language, your facial expressions, and your voice/instrument.

4. If you're a Singer, sing to someone in the audience, looking at them directly, for a few seconds, and then

someone else a few seconds. (This will often make them a fan for life!)

5. You can never afford to be "the genius" or "the Star", aloof and remote, no matter how great you feel you are, or may be.

6. Communicate!

H. Mistakes aren't fatal.

1. If you seem vulnerable or defenseless - they'll love you! Turn the error into an asset.

2. Don't be stuffy or exhibit anger because someone goofed - play it for fun.

Section 6:

Becoming Known

1. Getting A Gig: Performing

(Step 1 – Setting Up Your Promotion & Materials)

To many Singers and Musicians, there's nothing like performing before a live audience. But, "booking" takes work and is very competitive. There are countless others in the running, and your success, other than your musical skills, depends upon several important items.

*I recommend that, before you go any further, please read "**Addendum #2**" at the end of this course.*

    A. Professionalism is everything. Whether you represent yourself or have an Agent (or Manager) …

        1. You have to appear professional.

        2. You have to <u>be</u> professional.

My definition of "professionalism" is: Giving respect to everyone and everything regarding your career. This includes: your "team" (Artist, Manager, Musicians, Crew, Attorney, Agent, etc.), your Fans, your Music, yourself, etc., in every way possible.

For example, you're meeting an Agent: You, as Artist or Manager, are on time, you are fully prepared mentally and otherwise, you have a great looking "press kit" with a great sounding recording… You get the picture.

B. You need a Great, Professional looking physical (besides an Electronic - "**EPK**") "Press Kit" that fits your image. It should include...

    1. A "promo sheet":

        a. Should give Artist's background,

        b. Places played,

        c. Any interesting material, including biographies of the Band members, if worthwhile,

        d. It should be written well and neatly on a computer with your own "Logo" and design.

            (1). If necessary, use a great writer, or a professional publicity person and designer.

            (2). Someone else, like the Manager, can write more objectively than the Performer or Leader and might add some things the Artist may think are not important.

            For example, the Artist might have gained some notoriety in another entertainment or even non-related field that still would interest someone.)

    2. Great pictures are important.

        a. With so many people nowadays with Digital Cameras, someone should be able to produce some good pics. If the quality isn't there, hire a Professional. (You can also check out photography schools in the area). I recommend someone who specializes in entertainment photos.

b. Photos should contain, at least...

    (1). Act's name (And Manager's name if one exists)

    (2). Email and Mailing address, and

    (3). Phone #.

c. You should have at least:

    (1). One or more different black and white 8 X 10-inch photos and/or...

    (2). Four 4 X 5-inch prints may help you also, in an 8X10 frame.

d. Have new ones made from time to time to update Artist's image.

e. Request the negatives, or if digital, your copies on CD – if you paid for them, they're your property. They can be used to make quality, but less expensive multiple copies.

3. A *quality* demo recording on CD.

a. It should contain 3 - 5 of your best (Great!) Songs.

    (1). If Artist performs only Originals, it should be made up of Originals.

    (2). If "Cover Songs", only cover Songs.

    (3). If Artist plays both kinds, have one CD of each.

b. The sound should be the best you can get.

(1). It can be made during practice.

(a). If you don't feel the equipment you record with is good enough, beg, borrow or rent better equipment to make this recording.

(b). Make sure either you know how to set it up and run it, or have someone there who does.

(2). Consider making a live studio (direct to 2 track - not multi-tracked - you want a live type of sound) or live performance demo. (Refer back to "Sound Check" from Section 5)

c. A great CD can be very helpful in getting gigs - and a bad one can cost you any chance you may have.

d. Properly label the box! It should contain, at least...

(1). ... the name of the Artist

(2). ... the names of the Songs

(3). ... "The Copyright Notice" (if, original Songs). The Copyright Notice contains three elements in this order:

(a). The word "Copyright" (or preferably, the symbol " © ")

(b). The Year it was Copyrighted.

(c). The Owner's name (If Songs are not "Published", it's usually the Songwriter's name(s))

(4). Contact information: preferably the Manager's name, phone number and email address.

e. Properly label the CD itself (they always lose the box!) with at least a contact name and phone number!

4. If you have a great 3 – 5 song video of the Artist's best performances, all the better! If necessary, hire someone who knows what they're doing!

    a. The industry has become very, very bent on "Image" - that is, the way the Artist looks and comes across to his/her/their audience, visually.

    b. Video, even more than audio, can help you or hurt you. If you have a great one, use it. Otherwise, stick to audio.

    c. Video recordings can help you "play for" 5 agents/places at one time!

    d. You can play the Videos on your Web Site, Instagram, You-tube, etc.

5. More Successful Groups often have:

    a. Full-color press kits

    b. Posters

    c. DVDs

    d. Records/CD's/Tapes.

These may cost a little more, but indicates you're "successful". Appearance and image are very important!

6. Web Press Kits (EPKs) are now available so people can see them on-line.

Have these as well as the standard kits!

    a. Some people prefer online in advance of possibly meeting with you.

    b. People can see them on *their* timing.

    c. You make one kit, but many people can see them.

    d. It's more professional nowadays because it seems that you're "up with technology" which is becoming more and more important in the Music Industry.

2. Getting a Gig: Performing

(Step 2 - Action!)

A. When your press kit is complete, <u>use it</u>. If you have an Agent, go over it with him/her. Discuss where the Agent will take it and let them get started.

    2. Whether you represent yourself or not, make a list of people and places you are going to contact, including Agents. Start calling them, setting up appointments, and keeping them.

        a. Give your kits to:

           (1). Newspapers along with informative material about where you'll be playing, etc.

           (2). Booking Agents

           (3). Record Producers

(4). Clubs

(5). Managers (if Artist doesn't have one)

(6). Anyone else who may be able to help you

b. Don't forget to use your Electronic Press Kit ("EPK") that's on the Web. Put it on a site that hosts EPKs and/or on your own website. Send everyone a link to your EPK Web Sites, and place the link on your Instagram, Facebook, ReverbNation, Business Card, etc.

B. Get started! Go out & get gigs. Be just as creative in this area as the Artist is in theirs! Here are some ideas in no particular order:

1. What about clubs that don't usually have entertainment?

a. If they don't have room to perform, forget it.

b. If they do...

(1). Convince them you can bring people in.

(2). Make some kind of deal.

(3). Tell them you'll help promote it on your Web Sites!

2. What about clubs that usually "book" only on weekends?

a. Ask to come in on an "off" night and try to "build up the owner's business".

(1). Tell them you'll help promote with photos for the club and information for the papers.

(2). You might wind up being the weekend feature.

(3). Work on some kind of percentage of business.

(a). You can make some kind of income on a night when you usually don't work.

(b). How about half the "gate" or "cover charge"? The owner isn't putting out money but picks up some of the gate he wouldn't otherwise plus additional money on liquor and/or food.

Don't forget that it's "exposure" - The Artist is gaining valuable experience and getting "tight". Artist is also playing somewhere and being seen!

<u>Important Note:</u> *Show a Club-owner you can draw a lot of people and they'll be glad to have you back! Remember It is not (only) how good you are, but the number of people you draw that makes the owner like you! If they see you're great for business, you can even ask for more money the next time!*

3. What about "Showcases"?

a. Don't worry about the money - put on a great show and it will pay off in the long run.

b. Find a club-owner who'll let you use the place.

(1). It'll be great for the club having new people see their place.

(2). They'll make money from liquor and/or food sales

c. Make up an invitation list including:

(1). Club owners

(2). Booking Agents

(3). Entertainment writers and columnists from the local press

(4). Disc jockeys

(5). TV news and entertainment people

(6). Managers

(7). Recording people

(8). Anyone else who might be able to help you in any way

d. Let them in for free.

e. Have a photographer & video person present.

f. Have some kind of great, fun food and drinks.

g. Talk to everyone, but don't hit them with "hard sell".

h. Have fun yourself, and make sure everyone else does.

i. Be sure to invite some of your friends as well as the other people.

This is one place where friends and relatives can definitely do you a lot of good - helping to pack the place!

4. What about the college circuit? There are agencies that do nothing else but book Bands and Performers for schools and colleges.

5. Don't overlook any opportunity to gain exposure. Think about, for example:

Open-Mic nights, TV... Radio... Cable... hotels... restaurants... fraternity and sorority socials... Bar and Bat Mitzvahs... block parties... school dances... local celebrations, weddings and receptions... festivals...shopping mall events... conventions... fashion shows, malls etc., etc., etc.

Even if, at first, you play for less than you want - do it! You can build up a following which will open many doors! Plus you'll get your show tight for the "Big-time"!

6. Don't forget the Internet

   a. Many venues have their own Facebook, etc.

   b. Mention on your sites that you're looking for booking

   c. Send out Bulletins and other electronic "flyers" to your Internet friends telling them to help you out.

   d. "Stream" your songs on your sites so people can hear you. I know of many, many acts that have gotten gigs because agents heard their stuff on YouTube, etc.

3. Promoting your Act:

Important: *The greatest talent in the world is worth nothing if no one knows about them and/or their products!*

A. Proven ways to promote your act (in no order - they're all important!) are...

1. Word-of-mouth from gigs and recordings - there's nothing like it! It means you're so great and unique and marketable that people are constantly telling other people about this "Great act" they heard or saw! It becomes a chain-reaction: people telling people telling people. . .

2. Have a Great press kit. Be sure information and pictures go to the newspapers, including local weeklies or dailies that cover the section of the city where you're playing.

3. Place Posters/flyers/hand-outs around town aiming for places where your (type of) audience will frequent.

4. Get on a radio disc jockey show or a local "talk show" to showcase your act playing Songs and/or talking about your act, etc.

5. Get on a TV talk show.

6. Have an "e-mail / Face Book list"

   a. Get people to sign up at gigs or wherever, at least their 1st name and email, and if possible, their phone number, for texting.

   b. Come up with all the names and addresses of people that are, or might be, interested in hearing you.

   c. Get and put up a "widget box" on your sites where people can sign up.

7. Have a Newsletter – an e-zine/e-mail - and periodically send out a newsletter discussing...

   a. Gigs coming up

   b. Gigs you've played

c. Interesting events Artist's been involved in

d. Interesting stories about the members

e. Recording updates

f. Merchandise for sale

g. And, of course: Where the Agent or Manager can be reached for bookings or other things.

8. Have a Fan Club / "Street Team".

a. It can generate a lot of talk & energy

b. It can provide bookings through the efforts of one or more fans.

c. Encourage the fan club people to let the media know they exist. Great publicity about a fan club reflects well on the Artist.

d. Carefully pick the right person to run it. Make them feel special - (Artist's names involved.) Choose someone who's...

   (1). Enthusiastic

   (2). Efficient

   (3). Businesslike

   (4). Trustworthy - they're handling money

   (5). Totally responsible.

<u>Remember</u> - *The important thing to fan club members is the recognition they receive from the focus of their admiration - the Artist! Make them feel special and pay them if you can.*

.

9. Design/get Tee shirts (and other products w/Artist's name and/or Logo and Picture). Come up with some unique items that fit your image.

   a. Sell them to your fans at gigs and through the Fan Club.

   b. Send free samples of all the products to all the media, radio, TV and newspapers.

   c. Sell them through your Web Sites.

10. Have owners & Managers of clubs you're playing advertise you. Offer to help them!

11. Use the Entertainment Section Listings of newspapers.

   a. They need dates at least two weeks in advance, usually.

   b. Listings in entertainment sections are news and should cost you nothing.

12. Get Local writers or columnists to write you up. Come up with a great "hook"! Just like Songs need great hooks - so does promotion. Examples:

   a. Funny or interesting things about Artist.

   b. How you got started.

   c. Your unique "Show".

d. Other Entertainment Business highlights.

e. Interesting Hobbies.

f. Whatever! Find something!

13. Use Radio and TV shows available. For example:

a. "Public Interest Announcement" segments.

b. "Community Bulletin Boards", or "Entertainment Updates" where your play dates can be announced.

c. Radio promotions, where, for example, you work in conjunction with a station promoting you and the station.

14. How about: Independent TV stations and Cable TV?

a. If you're great, or highly visual, or unusual, they might be interested in taping you live in performance. They're always looking for something unique and interesting.

b. Do you use unusual instruments?

c. Do you use comedy?

d. Do you have a great and/or unusual Light Show?

e. Some Cable TV stations allow you to put on your own show!

(1). You can sell advertising time to pay the costs...

(a). To music, music equipment and/or audio stores,

(b). Clubs, other businesses (some of whom may have taped TV spots they'll buy time for on your show), or...

(c). You can just plug yourself and your merchandise that's for sale.

(2). If you're lucky, you can make a few dollars.

(3). More importantly, this should give you a great demo or video plus important experience.

15. Have a great Website! This is very important - a necessity!

a. Have a great web designer design it, making sure it fits the image you wish to project!

b. Put up pictures of Artist (by using a Scanner or Digital Camera)

c. Include everything that you can to promote the Artist, including, but not limited to...

(1). Interesting facts

(2). Sound snippets

(3). Future gigs

(4). Bios

(5). Ways to contact Artist and Management such as their e-mail addresses

(6). Your EPK (or link to it)

16. "Social Community" Web Sites such as Face Book, ReverbNation, etc....

 a. Attract "friends" to your site - and You and your products.

 b. Attract people to other sites that contain you and your products.

 c. Some performances

 d. EPK Links, etc....

 e. Stream some of your songs

17. Give a Private VIP party we discussed earlier!

18. Keep a scrapbook to show people just like you show your "kit".

19. If signed to a Music Publisher, Record Company, etc.

 a. Make sure they promote you well.

 b. Have what they intend to do spelled out and agreed upon in your contract.

20. Hire someone to handle your promotions. There are skilled people available who have the personality and know-how to push you well, and who have connections you might never make on your own.

 a. Look at promotions they've done.

 b. Ask for references, talk to the people, and try to establish their competence.

c. Ask about a trial period, 3 or 6 months, and put it on paper.

d. It's possible (but unlikely - unless they need to get started!) they'll work on some kind of percentage of the profits plus expenses, or some kind of swap.

21. If you are or have a Manager it's one of the Manager's most important jobs!

a. They should take care of most or all of the promotional work mentioned above.

b. It's more professional to have someone other than the Artist be the promotion person!

c. If a separate promo person is hired the Manager should deal with them.

d. The Artist should be called in only when something relative to a promotional appearance is necessary.

Important: *The Fans want to talk to the Artist – not the promo person, Manager, Attorney, etc. It is very important nowadays for the Artist to talk to their fans on their social networking sites, via email, etc., besides in person!!!*

Also keep in mind that the Artist must never forget that they're promoting themselves 100% of the time by the way they are in public. They mustn't defeat promotional efforts in their behalf. The public's devotion, which can be strong, is fickle at best, and if the Artist doesn't come across the way the public perceives their "image" to be, the Artist's career may suffer.

Section 7:

How to Record an Artist

The decisions you make regarding Recording are just as important as when Writing, Practicing & Performing - every step in the music business is just as important as the others! Your Name is on the line – and how you sound is very important when aiming to make a great "1st Impression"! It's important to keep in mind that the Music Industry has changed so much through the last 20 years that it's hard to separate the difference between the Songwriter, the Arranger, and the Producer - what each is responsible for. Simply put:

A. Songwriter: The Song = Words & the lead singing notes.

B. Arranger: The Arrangement = Background voices, instrumentation, chords, tempo, rhythms, etc.

"Beat Makers" actually fall under the category of "Arranging", though they usually consider themselves Songwriters, and call themselves "Producers". This situation comes up mostly in Hip Hop and R&B, and some Pop.

C. Producer: The Production = Overseeing the Recording process up to, and including the final mixing of the volumes, effects, panning, of the instruments and voices, etc., and even okays the final "Mastering", where it's ready to be duplicated and released.

1. Pre-Production

A. Decide what kind of recording you should make - from one instrument to a "Master" (finished Recording ready for marketing). It depends on...

1. What's the purpose of the Recording?

   a. If it's for gigs - a good clean "live" recording should suffice, recorded at gig or very simply at a studio – straight to 2 tracks.

   b. If you are going to sell it yourself it should be a great finished recording - preferably a "Master."

   c. If going to a Producer, Manager, or a Production Company, ask them what they want or will accept.

   d. If going to a Record Company, or you're putting the recordings out yourself; that is, selling them at gigs and placing them on the Internet, you should aim for a complete, ready-to-go Master.

2. What's your "aim" when Recording?

   a. The Artist and Songs must come across. That is you must really grab the person, company and audience's complete attention with this recording.

   b. A person should be able to sit back and just "Feel the Artist and Songs" without any music or sound-related distractions.

   c. No overplaying, long intros, non-fitting parts, too soft vocals, poor sound quality, or heavy "hiss" or other noises

   d. The Recording must be great enough to really show the Songs and Artist in their best light.

B. How many Songs should be on the recording?

   1. For Gigs and for general showing: 3-5 songs

a. "Cover Band": 3 - 5 of your best-performed Songs

If you wish to release a cover song, you must get a "License" from the Publishing Company – that is, the owner of the Song. This also includes using "samples", plus, you'll need to have permission from the Record Label, also, with samples.

b. Original Band: 3 – 5 of your strongest, best performed originals

2. For Record Companies: 3-5 of your strongest original Songs

For gigs, it also helps if you have live recordings with the crowd cheering, too!

C. Regarding picking and recording the right Songs

1. Pick your strongest material: You don't get a 2nd chance to make a 1st impression!

Let Music Biz people help you with this. Ask for their opinions... The most popular songs at shows, don't always translate to songs with potential in the recording industry, and vice versa.

2. Is the material appropriate for where you want to send or take it?

D. Who is going to play and Sing the Songs?

1. What Instruments & how many Musicians do you need?

2. Will you need background Singers?

3. If you have a great, self-contained Band - great!

4. Is someone (Musician/Arranger/Producer) supplying you with finished "Tracks"? (Note: see Section 3 below re: **Home/Preproduction Studios**)

E. How do you choose the right Musicians/Singers for your Recordings?

    1. As people:

        a. Do they have ego problems?

        b. Can they be part of a team?

        c. Do they have a professional attitude - time is money!

    2. As recording talent:

        a. Are they good enough?

        b. Do they like the Songs they will have to play or Sing?

        c. Can they feel the material?

        d. Try them out before recording sessions - see how they mesh with what you have in mind.

F. Singers: (Both the Recording Artist and Background Singers)

    1. Do they have a "wall", that is, do they communicate when they perform? They have to be "real", "sincere", "natural", and be able to lose themselves in the Songs. They must have no fear of showing their inner feelings.

    2. Their enunciation should be pretty clear.

G. Musicians: (Both the Recording Artist and added Musicians)

1. Must play from the heart - with FEELING - not "mechanical" sounding.

2. Must be able to keep it simple - The right note in the right place.

    a. No overplaying - especially when the singer is singing - except in certain situations toward the end of a Song.

    b. The musical "spaces" (where nothing is played) are important!

    c. They should never get in the way of the Song!

    d. Their job is to bring out the Song - help create a mood.

Think of movies: If done well, you feel the tension, or whatever from the music, but you don't necessarily "hear" the sound – it doesn't take your mind away from what's happening – it just enhances it.

3. Can they play on time?

4. Musical hooks are very important!

5. Should play in consistent patterns, not varying too much. For example: What they play on verse #1 = verse #2; chorus 1 = chorus 2, etc., while slowly building, sometimes with an additional part appearing.

H. Are other people needed? Are you going to play the part of, or are you in need of, a...

1. Producer? (Equal to a Director of a Movie)

a. In charge of directing whole procedure

b. Chooses the "Right Songs"

c. Makes all the necessary changes

d. Sets up studio and sessions (may have own studio or access to one)

e. Gets the best possible recording

f. May arrange/play the "tracks"

g. Why hire a Producer?

    (1). Experience

    (2). Can be more objective

    (3). Buffer zone with other all the personalities/ members

    (4). Connections (for a "price", of course - usually wants "part of the deal")

2. Engineer? Do you prefer your own, or the one that "comes with the studio"?

3. Arranger?

4. Programmer?

a. Programmer is responsible for running musical computer programs involved with the arranging and producing of your music.

b. If it involves "Digital recording" or "Sound Designing" you will need one.

c. If you are doing solely analog (tape), you shouldn't need one.

(See Section 3 below re: **Pre-production Studios**)

I. How are you going to pay for these people?

1. Money.

2. Other deals or exchanges of help or whatever.

3. Use your imagination: Examples:

a. Mention their name on Recordings - they can use Recordings to make advancements with their Career.

b. Open some of your connections to them (be careful - your name's on the line!!!)

Though you may find the following types of studios in one place, I'm separating Standard Studios, (directly below in #2), from #3, which are often called Preproduction or MIDI studios, (which are often found in someone's home, or another section of the Standard Studio's facilities).

2. Where to Record (Regular, Standard Studios)

A. You must decide which Recording Studio is right for you.

1. Find a studio that can give you what you need! Your aim being, a studio that produces very high-quality product, in a comfortable working environment.

2. The Best That You Can Afford.

B. Next:

1. Tell your musician friends and other people in the Industry that you're looking for a studio.

    a. Telling them what you need to do, and the amount that you can afford.

    b. Ask them where they recorded and about the quality of their recordings and their experience.

    c. Listen and decide with your own ears, and make your own decision.

2. Check out these places and other places you hear about or find on the Web, and then choose a few studios that make sense to you.

    a. Make an appointment.

    b. Visit them.

    c. Talk to them, explaining what you want.

    d. Listen to the recordings they've done of other people.

        (1). If possible, listen to Recordings in your style of Music.

        (2). The recordings should sound clean, crisp, and have great tonal quality without hissing or cracking. That is, there should be no annoying sounds.

        (3). Ignore what that Artist/Group sounds like, unless their Producer is the one you want. It doesn't matter if they are good or bad - just focus on the recording quality.

e. Talk with, and go over their equipment with the Engineer who will be working with you.

(1). Ask questions no matter how dumb you think the questions or your concerns, are.

(2). Make sure the engineer you'll be working with, is one you can work with!

(3). An engineer should only do what you ask them to do.

(a). They shouldn't take over the session.

(b). They should be willing to offer suggestions if asked - they know their equipment better than you do.

C. Equipment: What's necessary?

1. Great (and a variety of) Microphones.

2. Larger and small speakers.

3. "Outboard gear" (Computer program and/or "stand alone" hardware units).

At least:

a. Noise Reduction units,

b. Compressors, Expanders, Limiters,

c. Reverbs, and

d. Digital Delays.

4. Depending on your situation: Keyboard Synthesizers and "Sound Samplers" with plenty of "sounds" and Computers with up-to-date Programs. (And people that know how to operate them, unless you do.)

D. Most studios have a list of people such as: Songwriters, Arrangers, Producers, Musicians, Singers, and others. Make deals directly with the individuals, if possible, that you need.

E. Find out what the studio is and is not responsible for.

1. They should be responsible for:

a. Providing well-maintained and functioning equipment.

b. A knowledgeable Engineer (and Programmer where applicable).

c. Holding backups/originals of your Recordings safely.

d. You should not be charged for the time involved when equipment is malfunctioning or for Engineer/ Programmer mistakes.

2. Studios are not responsible for:

a. Wrong production decisions made by you or whomever you personally hire.

b. Time wasted by the client or the client's associates.

3. Where to Record (Computerized – Home or Pre-Production Studios)

Although anyone can sometimes record at these computer-centric studios (even complete bands if there's enough room), Pre-Production studios are especially important if you are a Single Artist or Vocal Group; that is, you are not a self-contained band. You can do most of the work yourself, with little additional help, or most likely the Studio person can do the work with or for you. Do keep in mind that, a good amount of these Studios are "Pre-Production" Studios, and they don't necessarily have the ability to make finished Masters.

A. Why use a Home-like studio?

    1. If you don't know of any Musicians that:

        a. Can do justice to your Artist or Songs.

        b. Can play the Songs the way you want them played.

        c. Are reliable.

        d. Have great equipment.

        e. You can afford.

    2. Or:

        a. You want total control of the Recording.

        b. You don't want to deal with a lot of people.

        c. They are usually less expensive in hourly cost.

        d. The atmosphere is often more intimate. The studio may be in one comfortable room, maybe even in a house, with just you and the studio assistant present.

B. Usual Recording Equipment found in Preproduction Studios:

1. Sequencers to record your instruments. Sequencers can be:

a. "Hardware" (physical product) to be attached to your synthesizer/computer.

b. A "software" program built into your instrument.

c. A program for a computer, such as "Pro Tools". (You can record vocals through most Computer Recording Programs)

2. Most Professional Sequencers can:

a. Record most or all of your tracks.

b. Correct your timing.

c. Slow down the speed, play the part, and then speed it back up.

d. Record small parts (sequences) of the Song in any order.

e. Change the instrument later - (records data not instruments).

f. Record extra parts and pick the ones you like the best.

g. Computer versions of all types of outboard effects, plus totally virtual ones.

h. And much, much more!

C. Other Equipment and instruments:

1. Keyboards/Synthesizers

2. Keyboards/Sound-Samplers

3. MIDI capability (or Multi Instrument Digital Interface - allows all keyboards, computers to work together in sync)

4. Perhaps some physical outboard gear.

Caution: *These instruments run by skilled personnel are absolutely fascinating, but don't get caught up in it and get carried away. You have but one objective - A Hit Song! D. Ways you can save money:*

1. If you own a synthesizer or a sampler, or a Program with sounds, you can pre-pick the sounds then bring your instrument (or Program - if they don't have the one you're using) and patches/sounds to the studio - if they have the same instrument - and use theirs.

2. If you have a sequencer, especially a computer program that can give you compatible files, such as, .wav, you can possibly record the parts at home to "dump" into their system.

E. Important:

1. Have a meeting to know what the studio and personnel can and will/won't do.

2. See what equipment they have.

3. See what options you have.

4. The total cost. Are there any hidden costs?

5. Make sure that it's clear what you'll need, and whether they have the means to accomplish what you wish.

F. Do It Yourself. It might be worth buying:

1. A professional synthesizer or two with some great "sounds".

2. A sequencer.

3. A great mixing board.

4. A Computer/Program system to record vocals, provide sounds and effects, and to "Mix" the parts together.

Remember: You must learn the technical end and programming of your equipment and/or computer or hire someone who knows how to use it if you wish to do things yourself.

4. The Cost of Dealing with Any Studio

A. Cost factors:

1. Are you self-contained (or do you need Musicians, an Arranger, Producer, backup Singers, special effects, added synthesizers)?

2. Cost of any materials and the studio.

3. Be realistic. Figure what you absolutely need to get what you want accomplished.

4. List all expenses.

B. If cost is by the hour, the studio time charge begins immediately at time agreed upon.

1. Can range from $10 to $250 per hour and more. - even if no music is recorded!

2. Figure out in advance how much time you'll need for:

   a. Rhythm tracks

   b. Vocals

   c. Over-dubs and/or "sweetening" (like strings, horns, etc.)

   d. Mixing

   e. Making copies

3. Important: Always over-estimate!!!

4. The cost per hour usually depends on:

   a. Number of tracks offered or needed

   b. Quality/quantity of the equipment

   c. Studio's location

   d. Their prestige

   e. The amount of un-booked time available

5. Remember the price of tape (if recording "analog"):
Size of tapes needed - unmixed and mixed copies;
analog/DAT; 2 inch; 1 inch; maybe one-half inch tape 16

Smaller size track machines may have adequate quality for your needs and the tape cost is less.

6. Important: find out what is and is not included in the price. Make sure there aren't any "hidden charges".

7. Most studios have "package deals" or will set up one for you.

    a. Studios would rather have something going on than nothing happening.

    b. "Cash up front" can sometimes lower cost.

5. Preparing to Record

A. Good preparation:

    1. Sit in on other people's sessions if you can. (Ask Artist/Producer if you can, first!)

        a. It will give you a "feel" of the place, instead of going in "cold".

        b. See/hear the equipment/people who may be working with you.

    2. If you have a Band, rehearse the Songs without the vocals.

    3. Get used to working with headphones.

    4. Make sure the arrangement of the Song is the way you want it. Studio time is too expensive for practicing or making decisions you could have made in advance.

B. Make a list of things you'll need to have at the studio.

C. Don't bring extra people - it adds confusion, at the least.

D. Don't plan on doing everything in one day.

E. You want to have a great mental attitude. You want to feel confident. Being confident of the outcome is important. To ensure this:

1. Be prepared to record, making sure all the details have been handled.

2. Rehearse everything you must do.

3. Go over all performance details with the others who may be involved.

6. Recording your Song(s)

A. If Performing - Let yourself loose!

1. Sing and play from your heart. Otherwise the Recording will sound "mechanical".

2. Don't worry about making mistakes.

a. If you make a mistake, make a big one. You can always rerun the track and do it over.

b. Some mistakes are better than what you planned, so keep playing.

c. You can almost always "punch in" – that is, redo just the "bad part."

3. Maintain the same volumes on your instruments – it should be adjusted in the mix.

4. If using Analog tape and you see a shortage of tracks coming up, think about "bouncing" tracks" - mixing 2 or more tracks onto one track. But, the hazards are:

a. Once bounced - the originals are gone.

b. In effect, you are pre-mixing, and it had better be done carefully and well.

c. "Generation loss". (Loss of quality of sound going up and back using tape)

5. If something bothers you in the studio, sound-wise or otherwise, mention it to the Audio Engineer, Programmer, or Producer.

6. Caution: If you go on too long in a session, you may...

a. Become over-tired and your ears and brain will "burn out".

b. Make errors you wouldn't otherwise.

c. Not be hearing things accurately.

d. Make the wrong decisions about what to keep and what to erase.

7. I recommend, using separate days for...

a. Rhythm tracks

b. Vocals

c. Sweetening/overdubs

d. Mixing

8. This allows time for

    a. Adjustments in arrangements, etc.

    b. Avoiding burnout

    c. Just clearing your head.

7. Mixing

A. Clear out unnecessary people! This is the time for finished sound - what is going to be marketed - and critical decisions must be made without distraction.

B. Concentrate on producing a Recording in which the tones and volumes are such that the person listening will be able to sit back and feel it/enjoy it without having to concentrate!

C. Listen to and check your mix often through large speakers and smaller speakers.

D. Don't "overproduce" your material by adding too many sounds, effects, and whatever.

    1. Don't add anything unless it adds to the Song.

    2. Adding equipment adds noise. Often it is "felt" more than heard.

    3. An "under-produced" product is often easier to sell.

        a. The Music Biz People will hear what they want - the Song.

b. They'll foot the bill if they are interested in additions or changes to make the Song a "hit" (in their opinion).

E. Other people with "great ears" should listen to your mix

1. You've heard the Song a thousand times and probably have lost objectivity.

2. After they've heard the Song(s), ask them if anything "bothers them", and where.

3. Can they "feel" the Song?

4. Does it "take them somewhere"?
Remember, they are only giving you an opinion - not fact!

F. You are trying to capture a "special moment", one that stirs people and recreates that feeling each time they hear it.

G. Don't waste money trying to create the impossible. For example: trying to get a Master from a 4-track analog studio. Realize the studio's limits and what you may expect from it.

H. You're striving for an overall commercial, salable sound. Either the Songs and the Artist will come across, or they don't.

You'll notice my overemphasis on "The Song," over "The Artist". I'm sorry, but a Great Artist with a mediocre Song is going nowhere, unless the Record Company can hear something so, so very special in the Artist that they're willing to get the Songs from elsewhere for them. It's all about Hit Songs! Make sure Artist has top Songs - no matter what you have to do to write or get them!

Section 8:

Choosing and Dealing with Record Companies

Introduction: *With the state of the Music Industry so unstable, especially at the higher ends, I highly recommend, at least at first, that you start out playing the part of the Record Company, yourself. Even if you want to end up with a larger company, later on, there are major benefits to starting out on your own!*

It's also possible, if you start out on your own, and you are happy where you are, you may decide you'd like to stay where you are - with your own company. Or, meeting the situation halfway, you may be able to align your label with a larger label where they will do certain particular things for you, such as promotion, manufacturing and distribution, for example, kind of like a "joint venture.".

No matter what, even if you or your Artist has a set plan in mind regarding putting the Artist and their recordings out there, I recommend you read about all the scenarios.

1. The Record Companies

A. At this point you should have:

1. Strong Songs

2. Great Recordings

3. And you should know your Artist writes, sings, and performs really well.

B. Now it's time "to get yourself a Record Deal" (if that's what you're aiming for.)

1. The Manager, Agent, or perhaps an Attorney, will approach the Record Company and try to sell them on the Artist.

Nowadays, all Major Record Labels and their subsidiary companies will only accept a recording from successful Managers, Attorneys, and Producers. And will usually want the Artist to be at least fairly well-known, on their own, already. However, the Artist or their representative can still try to convince the Labels that they should hear them. Many of the smaller or more specialized Indie Labels will be more open to talking to you.

a. If you're new at the game, realize the worst possible thing that can happen is that the Record Company will "pass" - you'll be turned down.

(1). Realize it isn't the end of the world.

(2). There are other companies, plenty of them.

(3). The Beatles, Elton John, etc., etc., were turned down by all the companies at first.

(4). You might be turned down by 20 companies and on the verge of giving up, take a deep breath, go to the 21st . . . and become a star!

b. Lack of talent is not always the reason Artists are turned down.

(1). The Artist's particular talent might not appeal to a number of companies, but they still might eventually find someone who <u>does</u> want them.

(2). Quite often a company won't be interested no matter how good you are, because...

(a). They're overloaded with Artists at the time.

(b). They aren't doing your type of music.

(c). They have someone to whom you're too similar.

(d). The company has money problems

(e). And many more reasons...

2. Big Company or Small Company?

A. Big companies ("Majors" and "Mini-Majors" - Subsidiaries)

1. May be more prestigious, more powerful, and thus better able to do the best for you or your Artist.

2. They're geared to handling big productions and big promotions tied to big money.

3. If you're just "up and coming", they may believe in you but don't want to spend big money on you just yet.

4. Nowadays, they might want you to make it in the Minor leagues at first - such as with an Indie, including what you can do on your own.

B. Smaller companies...

1. May give you more personal attention and handle you well, up to a point.

2. They might produce a great Master Recording for you, but not have the money and power to promote it as well as it should be to make it "a hit".

C. The best idea is...

1. Don't make any decisions about your preference until you have thoroughly investigated different sized companies.

2. If you're "hot", the knowledge that you are comparing might cause a company to make a better deal just to get you.

3. Meanwhile, start out as your own Record Company. More on this later on...

CAUTION: *If a Record Company asks you for any money, for any reason, never, ever deal with them! A legitimate Record Company will put out the money for all recording sessions, promotion, etc.! Also, a legit company doesn't (need to) advertise! If they have an ad looking for Artists, or mail you something – ignore it!*

D. How do you start? Make an appointment by telephone.

1. Never mail your Recordings or other material to anyone you don't know, without at least speaking to them at first.

2. If possible, insist on an appointment, pleasantly but firmly, and be willing to wait a reasonable time to see the person.

E. TIP: most secretaries/assistants have pull with their bosses.

1. If they like you, they can influence the boss toward seeing you.

2. If they don't like you, or feel you'll waste the boss's time, you'll never get in.

3. Learn their name and don't forget it the next time.

F. On your appointment date:

1. Arrive on time and with every thing you need.

I recommend:

a. A neatly packaged and labeled USB, CD or DVD with 3 to 5 Songs.

b. Neatly typed lyric/word sheets.

c. Photos.

d. If you have a great press kit, bring it.

e. If you have any great videos on a DVD, bring it.

2. Once inside...

a. Smile confidently.

b. Say hello, or other small talk, etc.

c. Hand the package over and say something like "I'd appreciate you listening to my recordings."

(1). Don't over-talk. Let the Recording do the talking for you.

(a.) It's performance, not conversation that counts.

(b.) Never make excuses about the performance or Recording. (It puts negative thoughts into their head!)

(c.) Sit quietly while the person listens to it.

(2). Usually the first 15-20 seconds or so is enough for them to decide whether to listen further. (That's why you should have only a short intro!)

(a.) If it doesn't hit them, it's "fast forward" to the next song, and so on.

(b.) If they go back and listen to a particular Song, chances are that it interests him/her, for some reason.

(3). If your Recording is rejected...

(a.) Take it calmly.

(b.) Ask, "Would you tell me why you didn't like it or why you are not interested? I'd really appreciate knowing." Usually they will tell you, and that's all the better.

(c.) Don't feel bad; you've just learned something of value - at least in regard to that person or company.

(d.) Thank them and try to leave the door open for another try.

(e.) NEVER BURN BRIDGES! Be nice even though it may hurt!

G. What are the Artist's chances of getting a Major Deal? In descending order:

1. You have created a large "Buzz". Everyone's talking about the Artist. You're drawing lots of fans to your performances and selling lots of product.

The rest of the list is at least partially "subjective" – it's their opinion what is considered good and bad.

2. If you are an awesomely talented Performer and you have amazing songs, with a reputable Manager or Producer presenting you, your chances are pretty good that you'll at least be taken very seriously.

3. If you are an awesomely talented performer, and merely have pretty good writing, or vice versa, your chances are still pretty good.

4. If you are only pretty good at the above, your chances are remote unless...

a. You are pretty close to being really great at both writing and performing.

b. And you:

(1). Have a surefire "Hit Song" ... or,

(2). You possess some other unique quality, such as a neat image.

(3) You have a lot of fans

H. "Good" is not Good Enough! The stuff has to be GREAT!!!

Yes, I know, I listen to the radio, too, and I wonder why a good deal of those songs are being played when I hear much better ones on the "Social Media" Sites, etc. But you should always aim to be the best that you can be, anyway!

I. The Artist's work will most likely have to be sent in by a known Manager, or known Producer or Entertainment Attorney. Why?

    1. The Companies will usually only listen to these people because:

        a. The Companies had received so many bad recordings they figure, this way, an Attorney or Manager has screened it and this person presenting the Artist is willing to put their name behind their submission.

Managers and Attorneys won't (shouldn't) hand anything in unless the quality of the act is at least "in the ballpark."

        b. It's great business for the companies to keep lines of communication open with these submitters, because the presenter has - or will in the future - submit someone who is, or will be, a star that makes them money.

Section 9:

Making A Deal with A Record Company

1. Dealing with a Record Company

<u>Introduction:</u> *It is a fact that the entire Music Industry is in flux at the present time, and quite a lot of time is spent by/with the people and companies trying to cope with all the changes that are occurring. Let's look at dealing with "Record Companies", for example...*

I put Record Companies in "quotes", because, although the Majors and their Subsidiaries are still considered Recording Companies, nowadays the term "Record Company" may also include any Entertainment Oriented Company with tons of power and or money, such as what "Live Nation" did with U2, Jay-Z, Madonna, etc., for example.

Some of the newer types of deals are:

A. "360 Deals", where ALL avenues of income are included - including Performing, Publishing, Merchandising, etc.

B. "Joint Ventures", where everything is split rather equally with another Company.

C. "Up-streaming", where if you sell a certain number of downloads or sales by yourself or with an Indie, and a larger Company takes over many of the responsibilities at that point. Sales numbers, where you are "up-streamed" to a bigger Company, usually start at 50,000 copies.

... plus other variations that are coming into existence in the Digital Era.

My point is, although the long-time Record Contract options still exist, you need to be prepared for any and all options. It's another reason it is important for Artists, as well as their Music Business Managers and Entertainment Attorneys to be on top of everything that is going on.

(*For other helpful hints which will help you be fully prepared for everything, see Addendum #1:* **Before You Sign With Anyone...** *at the end of this course*)

A. Note: If/when you are offered a deal, even before you go to a lawyer, two things must be cleared up if the Artist is a Group/Band:

1. How will the Artist's royalties be split?

a. Is each member getting the same amount?

b. Are certain main people getting more, where newer "employees" are getting less, for example?

c. Are some "paid employees" (cash)?

2. How will Songwriter's/Publisher's royalties be split?

a. Are the actual Songwriters the only ones to receive Songwriting and/or Publishing royalties?

b. Will other members be listed and share monies?

c. Will Songwriter's get Songwriter's royalties and the other band members split the Publisher's share?

d. Etc.

*I think "c." above is a good compromise if the musicians contribute to the song, but are not getting any Songwriter's share and credit. (Please see my **Publishing Course** to get the full information re: Songwriters & Publishing)*

B. When a Company expresses interest in discussing a deal with you...

    1. Let them outline what they will do.

    2. Then, tell them you must discuss it with your Attorney and will get back to them.

C. Run to your Entertainment Attorney!

    1. If you don't have one, find a good one!

    2. Don't try to handle things yourself.

    3. The larger, legit companies will not deal directly with the Artist, anyway - it can cause problems down the line.

    4. Remember the Company has its own lawyers to handle negotiations and you're entitled, whether you're the Artist or the Manager, to the same thing.

    5. It removes you from the firing line.

    6. The contract you wind up with will probably be decided between their lawyers and yours, anyway!

    7. You may believe that money is the most important thing to be negotiated; your lawyer knows it isn't.

        a. It's <u>the way</u> you get the money.

b. The Record Company may bounce big figures around in front of you, and your objectivity may be lost.

Note: You RARELY will see any money from a Major Label after your initial "Advances", if any (except for Recording Costs' Advances)...

8. Your Attorney may...

a. Get you less money up front than you want - or they'll give.

b. But in doing this, may be able to substantially improve the royalties you will be paid, as well as other concessions.

9. Actually, the most important thing to be concerned about is "promotion".

a. Promotion is the major contributing factor to the way your Song or Albums/CDs do sales-wise.

b. Be sure your lawyer gets as much promotion as possible for you. It's rarely mentioned in the contract.

10. "Legalistics" are confusing at best so... Make sure your lawyer explains everything to you and that you understand it.

D. If the Artist doesn't have a Manager by this time:

1. The Record Company will usually refer or "recommend" one - who should be checked out by your Attorney - or...

2. May seek to have you sign with the Management Section of their Company, if they have one. The Management Section should also be checked out by your Attorney.

Be careful of this - make sure they (as Managers) are a larger company with the staff and know-how to work with you and represent you re: working with the Record Company. It can be dangerous, also - how can your Manager push the Record Company - if the Manager IS your Record Company?

Also keep in mind that nowadays, due to their lack of personnel, the Majors will probably insist you sign with a "Super Manager" who can handle a lot of work that the Labels used to handle.

a. The Record Companies feel more secure if they have control of your Management. It gives them better and more organized control of the project. They can...

(1). Coordinate tour support.

(2). Arrange live gigs to push record sales.

(3). Possibly get you more exposure on Radio and TV.

b. This can be good for you and them, because, for example, they gain more clout with Booking Agents and Concert Promoters by saying, "OK, if you want that act, you have to take this one, too."

E. Keep in mind that, if you are already an established Artist, your deal will move much faster. Reasons:

1. Most points will have been discussed beforehand.

2. The contract won't be a standard form and will have less to be argued about.

3. It won't be put on the back burner - they don't want to lose you.

F. There are four basic ways that an Artist will sign to a Recording Company:

   1. Directly to the Recording Company.

   2. Indirectly through an Indie Label (possibly your own).

   3. Indirectly through an Independent Producer/Production Company.

   4. Indirectly through a Music Publisher

Section 10 contains more about Production Companies, and dealing with them.

2. Important Deal Points:

The Direct Route: that is, the Artist is signing directly to the Record Company, with the understanding that there will be differences depending on the size and power of the Company, and how badly they want you...

Personally, I Highly Recommend the Artist doing it on their own, at 1^(st), where the Artist signs to their own Label, and then, if it's really worth their while, signs to a Major through Their Own Label),

No matter what, it's important to give you the following info, so as to give you a general picture of how a Major Label usually has been trained to think & act.

The Good News: Nowadays, the Major Labels have been forced to be more open minded, and many of the contract terms are often more negotiable than they were before. But only to a point – it mostly depends on how successful you've become on your own),

The Bad News: The contract language can still be very confusing, and definitely should be looked at by an up-to-date Entertainment Attorney.

The new Artist initial draft of a contract with a "Major" or "Subsidiary" may be up to 80 pages or so, with about ¼ of them covering the "deal points". The other pages aren't open to too much discussion - they're basic to everyone (called "boilerplate").

No matter what, most Record Company contracts won't be fair to a beginning Artist. It's up to your lawyer (a knowledgeable "Entertainment Attorney", hopefully) to make it fairer for you.

A. Exclusivity:

1. All contracts between Artists and Record Companies are exclusive! This means you can't record for another company.

They put a lot of money in and won't let you also record for other companies. Two possible exceptions you can win are:

a. Permission to do jingles and non-conflicting side projects.

b. A "sideman clause" where you can be involved, such as be an accompanying Musician, or a "Featured Artist," with recordings on another Artist's Sessions or Performances.

2. You are signed individually, even if in a Group. Remember, if you are part of a Group, you cannot leave the Group and sign with another "Label" without a written release from your recording contract.

<u>Important:</u> *A written release is the only way to be sure you've been released from ANY contract!*

B. The Term (the length of your Contract):

1. In the 1970s and before, the usual contract was for one year, with The Record Company having the option of four additional one-year options. The total: 5 years.

2. Now, 99% of the time, the term "years" has been changed to "contract periods". Here's one example:

a. The contract will usually say something like the following (condensed into simple language):

"Artist will deliver an album a contract period, which is nine months, with the option of the Company to request a second album during that period."

You think, "Hey, 5 nine-month periods comes out to only 45 months, or less than 4 years!" Wrong!!!

Example: Say you sign a contract and start doing your album, which takes Artist 3 months. The contract will say that the nine-month contract period starts after Delivery of that album - "delivery" means acceptable to them! (your "period" is now up to 12 months.)

Then they have the option before that period is over to ask for a second album - that extends your period again. It then may take three months to finish the 2nd album and nine months for that contract period to end for that record.

Therefore, conceivably, each contract period can last 2 years (or more); so, at that rate, a 5-period contract can last over 10 years!

b. What can you do to try and shorten this? Here are three possible solutions (depending on how badly they want you, or your Attorney or Manager's clout:).

(1). Have the total number of albums reduced. Example: try to reduce 10 albums to seven or eight.

(2). Have the nine-month period, where they can ask for another album during that period, be reduced from 9 months to, say, 6 months to decide if they want to request a 2nd album.

(3). Have the nine-month period between delivery of that 2nd album and the expiration of the period be reduced.

c. Another option:

(1). There would be a seven-album deal with one album during each nine-month period.

(a). Albums #2 and #3 would be elected by the Company on the basis of individual options.

(b). Albums 4 & 5, and 6 & 7, would be a double album package. (In most contracts it says you can't do this - it must be negotiated in the contract).

(2). This idea would bring the contract down to almost half the amount of time that you'd have to serve that company under the initial contract's terms.

The examples I am giving are just a few of many, many possible ways to tilt the contract more in your favor. The trick is for your Attorney to be just as creative negotiating your contract, as the Artist is in creating Music...

C. Product:

"Singles" or "album deal"? Especially with dance and rap, and some Pop & R&B, singles deals are often used, nowadays, but many deals are still album deals.

1. If they request a single deal, and it's profitable, they will request more sides - and it becomes an Album Deal.

2. You might have a better chance of signing in this way. The Company will be more inclined to take a chance on financing a single than an album. (Less cost). But if your recording becomes successful, it'll be automatically extended.

D. Recording Costs:

1. All recording costs will be ultimately paid for by The Artist!

a. The Company will advance them to you and charge them to you as part of your "Advances" (up front) against your eventual "Royalties" (down the road, as from sales).

b. The costs include all parts of the recording process, plus mixing and mastering, paying the Producers, etc., etc., etc. EVERY cost even remotely related to Recording (even travel, lodgings, whatever, wherever)!

Your lawyer may be able to get a few things deleted.

2. To keep the costs down:

a. Be well rehearsed before you go in.

b. Know when a Song is done and go on to the next one.

c. You can possibly get a "recording fund structure". That is, the portion left over can be kept as part of your "personal advance" (which still must be "recouped" – that is, paid back).

Remember "inflation": What it costs to do an album this year may cost way more the next year. The structure should have increases each contract period.

E. Advances: (Usually occurs only with Major Labels)

They usually grow each option period. They also often rely on:

1. The enthusiasm of the Company, re: the Artist's potential.

2. The financial shape of the Company.

3. The Manager involved.

4. The "chemistry" between the negotiators (how they get along).

5. If the Artist is a Singer-Songwriter.

6. Record Companies previous bad experiences.

7. Astrological signs of the Artists and such (I'm not kidding!).

8. Whether Publishing is involved.

9. The royalties payable.

10. Etc.

F. Royalties: Physical Copies

Yes, Physical Sales, such as Vinyl, still exist, and actually have been growing fairly well due to the fact more money can be made through them.

> 1. Usually is the "net sales of albums sold in the form of disc records through normal channels in the United States."
>
>> a. It will often be listed as the "base royalty".
>>
>> b. The next 5 or 6 pages in the contract involving royalties are devoted to reducing that to a lower number.
>
> 2. You want a <u>minimum</u> of 12 percent of retail (or 24% if using wholesale!)

You will find out that the contract usually says that the Artist has the responsibility of paying the Producer and much more from their royalties!!!

> 3. Royalties, like advances, *should* increase as the contract periods go on – it rarely says so in the Contract. They usually can escalate in 2 fashions:
>
>> a. An increase in base royalty from album to album and contract period to contract period.
>>
>> b. The second is predicated upon sales. That is, as sales reach certain plateaus, such as "Gold", "Platinum", etc., the royalties (should!) go up.

<u>Note:</u> If you ask for 3a. & b., the Company will probably say "OK". Why? Simply because, if you're successful, it's worth it to them. If

you're not successful, they can drop you at any time! So, what do they have to lose? But you must ask them for this when you sign!

4. Now, how will your base royalty be whittled away by the Company for physical products ("mechanicals")?

a. It's usually based on 90% of physical records sold - figuring on breakage. This is out of date - make it 100% of records sold! (Good luck!)

b. Outside of US sales may be one-half of royalty rate - try to get more!

Current royalty rates you should try for are:

(1). US 100%,

(2). Canada 85-90%,

(3). Major foreign territories 66 &2/3 to 75%,

Note: Make sure that major territories at least include, the United Kingdom, France, Germany, Australia, Japan - & wherever else possible.

(4). The rest of the world - 50%.

c. "Packaging costs": They try to take 25% for packaging of CD's - it doesn't cost them that much anymore! Make sure you get no less a reduction than what you get for cassettes – if they're still making them (usually 15%).

d. Remember mail-order, sale of budget records, licensed use of your records, sales through record clubs, and premium sales. Your lawyer might be able to help a little on these points.

G. Digital Sales (Downloads) and Streaming, etc.

This is becoming a larger and larger source of income and have been fought over with lawsuits coming and going, basically involving Artists saying they are not being paid what they believe is fair. Artists say it's part of "Licensing" - usually listed as 50%-50% - and Companies, want to pay the regular percentage as if it was covering sales of CDs (mechanicals) where Artist gets, maybe 10-15%. As of now, the courts are siding with the Artists, and consider Downloads & Streaming as Licensing.

Licensing: Licensing is where you allow others to put out your products, and most often regards allowing your recordings to be leased to TV, Film, Video Games, Commercials, and the like.

Make sure your attorney is up to date on this and that you're covered as best as possible.

H. Videos

The Record Companies presently charge your videos against royalties, even though they're often used as a promotional tool. They will probably try to "cross-collateralize" – which means taking profits from a profitable source, to pay for a non-profitable source, such as with Videos.

1. What to try to do:

a. It is impossible (or next to it) to get the Record Companies to absorb all the video costs as promotion.

b. You may be able to split them with the Company, although your share will still be cross-collateralized.

c. If all costs are to be taken from the Artist, try getting half the costs only recoupable from video profits.

2. What control can you have over video costs?

   a. Whether or not to do a video. This won't fly - and shouldn't!

   b. Try to have approval of production budget, including fees and royalties to the Producer. It's hard to pull off, but worth a try.

3. Video Pay: Basically you (should at least) receive:

   a. 20% of the wholesale price on physical sales.

   b. 50% of "net receipts" on licensed uses.

   Videos have lately become an extremely important method of income, and it must be prepared for by your Attorney.

4. One thing you must do: Under the "exclusivity section" of your contract, make sure there is a provision where you can do motion pictures or other video things that MAY make money for you!

I. "Controlled Compositions" (You won't see these words):

1. A controlled composition clause states that, in respect of Songs "owned or controlled by the Artist" (that is, Artist is the writer and/or Publisher of the Song), a mechanical license for the use of such Songs will be issued by the writer for a royalty less than that required by the copyright act.

Record Companies insist upon a three-quarter statutory rate (last count: 6.825 cents, instead of the 9.1 cents as stated by the Copyright Commission)

2. Additionally, they "insist" upon taking the difference between the 6.8 and the 9.1 cents from Songs you record from your royalties that are NOT written by you that they have to pay the other Publishers,

This is hard to fight for, but at least have them pay for 12 Songs instead of the 10 listed in most agreements - Artist is usually responsible for paying the difference between the 10 and the amount of actual Songs on the Album to the Publisher from their own income!

J. Merchandising

It used to be that there was no "Merchandising clause", or the Company was willing to drop their share of the revenues from such, where your "name or likeness" was used for sale of services & products, such as "T shirts", etc.

No more! Matter of fact, some have even purchased merchandising companies. They try to pay you 50% of the net - here we go again with the word "net". What can you do?

1. Try to have it deleted, or at least limited.

2. Make sure the merchandising rights retained by the Company do not interfere with your ability to exploit your success as a personality in the very lucrative field of advertising. That is, your ability to appear in, or use your name and likeness in connection with, radio, television and print advertisements endorsing the virtues of commercial products such as sodas, sneakers, or whatever! Two problems could occur:

a. You may, for example, sign to do Reebok and your Company wants you to do Adidas. Think about it.

b. You don't want to have to go to your Company and ask for a favor. They might want something in return you don't want to give up!

K. "Approvals" – Usually involves "Creative Choices"

1. Your first draft of your contract will have the Record Company in total control. However, there are some things in your contract where you might be able to get control of, or at least "the right of approval".

"Right of Approval" means, for example, they want you to use "Producer A". You don't want to use him/her. So they then offer, "Producer B", etc., until one is agreed to.

It also works vice-versa. You may want to use a certain Producer, and they say no. Then you or they would pick another, until it's agreed to. This can work with everything below:

a. Choosing your Producer

b. Which Musical compositions to be recorded

c. The times and places of recording and video productions

d. The Picture and biographical material pertaining to the Artist

e. The final sound mix

f. The Album/CD covers, including the artwork

g. The Liner notes

h. Joint recordings (your recordings with other Artists)

i. The use of the Artist's recordings in connection with premiums (enclosed with sales of other Products)

j. Coupling the Artist's recordings with recordings by other Artists

k. Recording budgets

l. The cuts to be used as singles

m. Video Songs and scripts

Actually, the easiest way to keep creative control? Make it big on your own, so that if they want you they will be "forced" to allow you to keep creative control. Hey, at that point they'll figure, "if it ain't broke, don't fix it."

L. An "Escape Clause" *must* be inserted in the Contract, where, if the Recordings don't get released, or if in any way the Company isn't doing their job within a specific period of time, you will be released from your Contract!

Important Note: Most or all of the above Important Deal Points will usually appear in a Recording Company Contract, though they'll be written in different words.

Actually, the most important point of listing some of the above points is to get you into a particular way of thinking when you look at contracts, and how important every little word or part can mean. Also, remember two other very important matters:

1. A person you hire to look at your Contract must be totally into the Music Industry and how it operates, going into the 2020's.

2. And I can't repeat this enough: It's not only what's IN a contract that can hurt you, but also, and just as importantly, what has been left OUT of the contract, that if inserted correctly, can save your butt!

Section 10:

Independent Producers &
Production Companies
& Starting Your Own Record Label

1. Production Companies

While you may be looking for a recording deal, you may be approached by, or you may wish to go with an Independent Producer or a Production Company, hoping, usually, to be signed indirectly through them to a Record Company.

But what actually is a Producer's job? Simply put, the Producer is somewhat equal to the Director of a Film. He/she/they are responsible for the entire musical recording process - and nowadays, usually a lot more! Many like to stick their paws into *everything*!

Now, what's the difference between a "Producer" and a "Production Company?" A Producer is the creative entity, where the Production Company is the business entity for the Producer. The Production Company is somewhat equal to the Executive Producer of a Film. They are the businesspeople.

A Record Company, in simplified terms, is really what I call a "glorified Production Company". The difference is that usually the Record Companies that we have known about through the years, now act almost like a bank, in that they financially and people-wise handle the manufacturing and distribution, as well as doing the bulk of the Promotion for the Artist and their Recordings.

However, nowadays, with the changes in technology and the way the Music Industry has been "forced" to operate, many more people and companies are taking over their position.

A. If you run into an Independent Producer or Production Company who is:

1. Unknown,

2. Inexperienced,

3. Has no clout,

Good luck! Try to exhaust other avenues first before using this type.

B. If you run into a legitimate Independent Producer with:

1. A good track record,

2. Respect in the industry,

3. You like their style and you mesh with them,

That's great! You should be flattered one shows an interest and take his/her offer, seriously.

C. With an Independent Producer the money involved will not be like signing directly with a Record Company, and there will be little to no advance money.

1. Yet with their clout you might attract a label's interest.

2. If you sign directly with a Record Company, they will pay a certain amount to you.

a. With a Producer, monetarily, you'll have to share your advances and profits with them.

b. Also the Producer will seek 50% of the publishing monies.

Publishing is what often attracts the Producer to the risk of his/her time, money and effort.

What they *should* pay for is Artist's recording time.

D. There are a few basic Independent Production deal structures.

1. With one, you might think you were dealing with a Major.

a. You would sign a complete Recording Agreement with the Production Company.

b. Then the Producer would (try to) negotiate their own contract with the Record Company involved, promising exclusive use of their Artist to the Record Company.

c. The Producer benefits wherever it can do better with its deal with the company over your deal with the Producer, along with his Producer's "points" (usually between 3% & 5% depending on their involvement and clout).

2. Another deal you might run into is the "pass-through" deal.

With this deal:

a. The contract may state something like. . . "The artist will receive one half what the Production Company gets, but no less than so and so % of the retail selling price.

b. Therefore there's a floor to the royalty and a built-in escalation in the event the Producer has significant "bumps" based on the artist's success.

c. Regarding advances (from a Major), it could be:

(1). A fixed amount of dollars,

(2). Or a share of what remains after recording costs are paid.

You still will be responsible for all recording costs.

d. Essentially after that, being a pass-through contract, all the monetary provisions are passed through to you from what the Production Company signs to the company for.

e. Basically the pass-through format is:

(1). Simpler

(2). Cheaper

There'll be less attorney fees and more possible money for you.

(3). This is a more harmonious way to go. Less fighting with the person you'll be attempting to work with.

E. An independent production deal's major points to consider are:

1. A pass-through vs. long form

2. Try for recording costs "off the top"

3. Advances - do the best you can

4. Royalties - do the best you can

You need a "floor" (lowest a number can be) and an escalator (steps up) for the high end.

5. Publishing - Try to get at least half with a "co-publishing" deal.

    a. Make sure that your obligations as a songwriter end when the production deal does! (co-terminous)

    b. Make sure the publishing and record deals are not cross-collateralized against each other. (Money from a profitable source is taken to make up for a non-profitable source)

F. Make sure you have the right to approve the creative Producer who works with you in the studio, and the right to replace him if you don't have success with him.

Realize that the Record Companies might shy away from you if you are locked in with a certain Line Producer with no options to have someone else acting as Producer in the studio with you.

G. Make sure there is a "release clause."

A release clause is a provision, whereby if a record is not recorded and released by a major label, for example, or a subsidiary of such, within a certain amount of time, the production contract - and the publishing contract - automatically end.

H. You also want the ultimate right to approve the label deal (good luck), so that your attorney can check it out before it's "passed through".

2. Your Own Record Company?

Nowadays, taking into consideration how rapidly the music industry is changing, more and more people have either decided they don't want to go with an established Record Company, or they have been forced to show what they can do on their own before a Record Company may become interested. However, the following info is necessary whether you wish to go with a larger label, or you wish to do it alone.

A. Yes, you can own your own Record Company!

1. It will probably cost a minimum of several thousand dollars besides a master recording to get started.

2. It requires you to:

a. Make your own recordings, and

b. Do your own promotion, etc.

3. An Entertainment Attorney will give you all the details concerning protecting yourself through incorporation, etc.

B. I'll recommend just about the only way to go about it with a chance of eventually becoming successful on a large scale with a Major.

1. In actuality, a Record Company is a glorified production company.

2. All successful larger Record Companies have all the:

a. Persistence,

b. People, and

c. Power needed to make a song a hit.

3. What you'll need besides recordings and some money is a ton of ambition.

4. You should start out with at least some CD's or Vinyl to sell at concerts or give out for promotional reasons.

5. Your aim is to get as much publicity as you can by:

a. Performing.

b. Having your music played on the Internet - your Web site and others, especially the Musical and Social Networking Web Sites,

c. Getting radio, TV and press coverage.

d. Having it played in appropriate clubs by DJ's.

e. Getting "airplay" of your recording on radio.

f. A *Must* nowadays: Artists must sincerely communicate with their fans – making them feel important and part of the musical experience.

If you do really well, you will notice that an established Record Company or Distributor(s) may become interested in your recording! Or, powerful Investors.

6. Why go through all this and still have someone else involved?

There is no way, unless...

    a. You have enough money to invest in yourself and exist,

    b. And have a lot of well-placed friends...

    c. And an amazing team of people working with the Artist and Company.

    ...for you to have enough money, contacts and people to handle the promotion and marketing of a whole country, let alone the world, if you wish to reach the upper tiers of the Industry.

7. If you just want to be a local star, or have a "cult following", or no interest in becoming really famous on a large scale, that's up to you.

    a. But to be a huge national/international star, and

    b. And make the money that goes along with it,

    c. Without having a nervous breakdown,

    ...it's best that you let someone who has the capacity to handle it, handle it.

    d. Also, you'll be so busy learning how to properly run, a Record Company, that you won't have time to make music!!!

8. There *are* major advantages of having your own company for at least a while:

a. If you do well locally, you will probably get a much better contract with an established Record Company than you normally would have (if you wish, at that point, to go that way).

b. You will receive your own Production Company royalties. (If you paid for them – you own the Recordings!).

c. You'll be getting Music Publishing royalties (where a good portion of your money will probably come from).

d. You'll be able to keep more artistic control.

e. You may even be able to become a subsidiary of a large company. (Ex.: Pooch Records/Sony)

9. There have been many, many Major Artists who wanted to, or had to start out this way,

a. Some because they weren't considered "good enough",

b. Some because they were too "different",

c. And still others who just wanted to keep full control.

Having your own Record Company, at least at first, is an option you definitely should consider.

Note: **Addenda #1, 3, & 4** below, go deeper regarding how to do it all yourself... Also, Professor Pooch's "**Producing, Production Company & Indie Label**" Course, will spell it out in much more detail.

Addendum #1

**Professor Pooch's 3-Step Music Business
Career Plan of Action**
©2019 David J. Spangenberg

Text & Audio:

https://www.professorpooch.com/Music-Business-3-Step-Plan.htm

Addendum #2

Indie Acts and Drawing Fans
©2019 David J. Spangenberg

Text & Audio:

https://www.professorpooch.com/UnsignedActs.htm

Addendum #3

The State of the Music Business Address
©2019 David J. Spangenberg

Text & Audio :

https://www.professorpooch.com/music-business-address.htm

Addendum #4

The Artist-Owned Indie Label Series
©2019 David J. Spangenberg

Text & Audio:

https://www.professorpooch.com/music-indie-label-series.htm

Addendum #5

Artist & Managers and Getting a Major Label Deal
©2019 David J. Spangenberg

Text & Audio:

https://www.professorpooch.com/artists-managers-major-label-deal.htm

Please keep in mind that the Music Business is evolving at an insane rate due to the effects caused by the digital explosion and the Internet. To stay constantly on top of things is important in the Music Industry, so I highly recommend that you remember to check my Website and Facebooks, often...

The Author. . .

David J. Spangenberg
("Professor Pooch")
Music Business Career Guidance
Educator, Author, Consultant & Mediator
Entertainment Contract Specialist
Email: Pooch@professorpooch.com
Web Site: https://www.professorpooch.com/
Instagram: https://www.instagram.com/professor.pooch/
Facebook Biz Page: https://www.Facebook.com/PoochCast
LinkedIn: https://www.LinkedIn.com/in/professorpooch
Twitter: https://twitter.com/Professor_Pooch

Also By this Author

"God Didn't Create Alarm Clocks"

Both a Personal Development and a Career Survival Kit for the Arts which will enable you to gain highly valuable insight into yourself and others, as well as the all-important career knowledge to deal with any and everyone who will appear in either your personal life or your career.

The Professor's Amazon Authors Page:
https://www.amazon.com/author/professor_pooch

CPSIA information can be obtained
at www.ICGtesting.com
Printed in the USA
LVHW101355281120
672906LV00055B/1608